# The Hidden
# Question
# of God

# The Hidden Question of God

by

Helmut Thielicke

translated by

Geoffrey W. Bromiley

William B. Eerdmans Publishing Company

*Copyright © 1977 by Wm. B. Eerdmans Publ. Co.*
*255 Jefferson Ave. S.E., Grand Rapids, Mich. 49503*
*All rights reserved*
*Printed in the United States of America*

*Second printing, June 1978*

**Library of Congress Cataloging in Publication Data**

Thielicke, Helmut, 1908
    The hidden question of God.

    Translation of Die geheime Frage nach Gott.
    Translated and edited by G. W. Bromiley.
    1. Theology—Addresses, essays, lectures. I. Title.
BR85.T4813         231        76-44492
ISBN 0-8028-1661-4

Translated from the German edition, *Die geheime Frage nach Gott*,
by special arrangements with the publisher, Verlag Herder KG,
Freiburg im Breisgau. © Verlag Herder KG Freiburg im Breisgau
1972.

# Editor's Preface

This little work by Helmut Thielicke is made up of a series of addresses, articles, and chapters, along with a condensation of one of the sections in his work *The Evangelical Faith*, Volume II. In the collection the author offers a popular and readable introduction to his basic thinking without the clutter of academic apparatus. The book will be found especially profitable by Christians who wish to consider their faith in its relation to many issues in contemporary thought. But it could be equally useful to thoughtful people who, finding difficulties in Christianity, are yet prepared to look at modern issues from a Christian perspective. Especially persuasive is Thielicke's primary thesis that behind all the questions of the age the basic and ultimately authentic question, hidden though it may be, is the question of God.

It might be noted that in this English version a few editorial changes have been made which, it is hoped, achieve some shortening without sacrificing anything essential. For example, it has seemed best to follow consistently the more popular style of the early chapters and eliminate all footnotes, usually by their incorporation in the main text in much abbreviated form. Again there has been abridgment in places. This is especially true in the chapter on the question of God, since readers who want a fuller statement may in this case turn to the relevant section in Volume II of *The Evangelical Faith*. Elsewhere material has been slightly compressed which has a more restricted German reference.

On the material side, a change of order has been made. The treatment of the question of truth has been given independent status and placed before the discussion of the question of God. In this way the book moves to a more natural climax and conclusion when the hidden question is finally brought out into the open and given direct consideration and answer.

Geoffrey W. Bromiley

# Contents

# I

# The Question
# of Religion

## 1. Escalation of Interest

In journals, illustrated magazines, and other publications
we are constantly reading articles which leave the impression that religion is cramping, that dogma is out-
dated, that the historical Jesus has been reduced to un-
intelligibility by the church and stylized as a cult hero,
that science has drawn a violent line through everything
that is called supernatural or transcendent, and that under its influence the world has long since been established
as a self-resting finitude.

Many people accept this helplessly because they
neither know nor even sense what Christianity is all
about. If we do not know who popular figures of the day
are, we feel inferior in educated circles, but if we do not
know who Isaiah, Job, and Paul are, our ignorance might
win us a certain prestige. We have left such things behind
us. Quite apart from what we might be losing in the
process, we do not even seem to have an inkling—and this
betrays a true lack of education—of the normative role
of these thinkers in the shaping of our culture.

Do we have to be taught this by the Czech communist Gardavsky, who in his book *God Is Not Totally Dead*
tells us that the Bible is one of the books that one has to
have read if one is not to be poorer than other men?

To get to the bottom of this question I am going to
advance what is perhaps a surprising thesis. I get the
impression that in inverse proportion to the abandoning

of the church as an institution there is a contrary process, namely, a general escalation of interest in religious questions. Joachim Scharfenberg drew attention to this in a recent article on Bloch, Reich, and Fromm when he asked, provocatively, whether man is not incurably religious. A student in one of my projects bears it out when he says that "we are continually asked why we are Christians." An older person even asked him outright whether he was sincere or was simply taking part in a propaganda stunt. The student could show him from many examples that he was constantly confronted by this question. This corresponds to my own experience.

Naturally, the question: What is your attitude to religion? or: Why do you believe? is not always put directly. In conversations of this kind the terms God and Christ are not normally used. Ciphers have to be decoded to detect the religious interest. But if they are, one can find traces, for example, in the poets. I do not mean Christian poets here, but those who are out and out secular.

In Samuel Beckett's play *Waiting for Godot* (1954), for example, the God question is the true if hidden theme. For Godot (which intentionally echoes the word God) is the figure, the $x$ in the equation, on which everything hinges. If this place is empty, nothing makes sense. The two vagabonds who are the only characters on stage simply fool around while they are waiting for Godot. It is astounding that the public puts up with this endless and pointless nonsense and does not interpose with a rational argument or at least a cry to get on with it. But one is unable to do this. For if the appointment with Godot does not come off, if he does not turn up, the rest is meaningless. There can be no meaningful dialogue. The words are empty. They are robbed of their specific weight. Thus there is a hidden logic in all the empty chatter. Whatever is said does not count if Godot does not come. It has no more point than the gabble in Eliot's *Cocktail Party* in which people miss the real theme of life. Only Celia, plunged into despair by the emptiness of life, takes refuge in caring for the sick, where (to use the image) Godot shows up for her and her life takes on a new solidity in which words too regain their meaning.

One may naturally ask whether it is right to speak of religious themes here, since in modern terms they are not articulated as such but can only be read between the lines. If religion is the return to a final reality beneath our lives, and if without this return we are merely spinning airy nothings and moving away from the goal, then religious themes are certainly introduced by Beckett and Eliot.

The characters are not unlike biblical characters such as Job, for whom Godot (Yahweh) threatens to vanish. For is not God refuted and compromised if he blunders by letting the righteous suffer while scoundrels go free? What kind of a God is that who fails so terribly as a world ruler? What kind of a God is it in whom we can see, not higher thoughts, but no thoughts at all? Is he not like the old dodderer in Wolfgang Borchert's *Draussen vor der Tür,* who bewails the fate of men but has no idea how to help them and no power to do so?

It is here that men fall into the void, seeing nothing to point beyond the nonsense of fate or accident. Does not Mephistopheles finally triumph in Faust's last hour when he calls God in question and seems to be right? Does not even Faust's greatest achievement, the building of the dam and the changing of the sea into fruitful fields, still lie under the rule of futility and decay? Are we not denied anything that lasts, anything that brings life to fulfilment? Does not everything move in a circle as though it had never been?

This moving in a circle, this endless circular movement, is precisely what Albert Camus is talking about when he describes the routine of rising, going to work, four hours of work, a meal, another four hours of work, another meal, sleep, the same comfortable rhythm each day. But then one day the question arises: Why?; and with this boredom, in which astonishment is mingled, everything begins.

Again we are reminded of a biblical figure who is frustrated by the same boredom and finds life a dead end. I am thinking of the rich young ruler who comes to Jesus and says: "Master, what shall I do to win eternal life?" (In other words, what is final and lasting?) The boredom which afflicts him is that he finds no basis in life, nothing which can be called absolute, nothing to make life worth living. He has looked for this. He has not just done so theoretically by investigating the meaning of life. He has done so very practically by involvement and action. Thus he has put his life under the discipline of God's commandments. He has tried the recipe of the church, which ought to be able to show man a goal which is more than a functional goal of the daily routine. But this has not helped him. Eternal life—life which is more than dull vegetating and which has an evident goal—has eluded him. Hence he comes in despair to Jesus. I need not tell the rest of the story, which may be found in Mark 10.

I simply want to stress one aspect, since it is connected with our present theme. When the young man confesses his boredom and emptiness, we read that Jesus looked at him and loved him. The statement of Camus is that everything begins with boredom mingled with astonishment. Here in the gospel it may be seen why everything begins thus, why there is a new beginning at this low point. It is because there is someone there who loves us. This love seeks the one whom it loves. It is always on his track. It is near to grasping him when life becomes painfully questionable and we ask despairingly: What is the point of it all?

Some might in sheer boredom take refuge in drugs. They might conjure up an imaginary world of mere appearance, a world which finally transcends and dissolves the empty round of the daily treadmill and the inanity of the welfare society. But even when they wander into the

dead alley of pot, that love recognizes the secret and unhappy cry for the reason and point of things. In the very
defalcation it sees the seriousness of the search and the
dignity of people who are resolved to break free.

Augustine once said that he could not seek God
unless God had already found him. One might add that
we are already found, that in terms of that gospel story
we are already loved, even when we do not expressly seek
God, even when we have let slip the very name of God
and substituted other ciphers such as the why of Camus,
or his alarm at the absurdity of existence, or nihilistic
despair, which is conceivable only as we make on life a
claim for basis, goal, and meaning.

But is this only a claim which I make on life—perhaps a desperate and hopeless claim—or does there stand
over my life an address which precedes all my seeking,
an address in the sense of the biblical saying: "I have
called thee by my name, thou are mine"? We are called
by our names long before the name of God comes back to
us. We are found even while we are still in the midst of
boredom.

This was my point when I said at the outset that
we have to decode the ciphers if we are to see how strong
the religious question is even where the word religion
plays no role or has even dropped out of circulation. My
next task will be to offer some instances in which the
religious question may be seen.

## 2. Alienation

The religious question may be seen in the thesis of the
alienation which usually results from manipulation, adap-
tation, and social pressures. Behind this thesis lies the
question of authentic man and the authentic nature of his
existence. But this question as to the ultimate meaning of
life is again a religious question, as is also the challenging
of the state of the world by utopian dreams. For in all
this what is sought is something that escapes empirical

apprehension and technological mastery. In the sphere of research and manufacture we are perfect and yet fundamentally we are terribly helpless.

A first decoding of these religious ciphers may be seen in Einstein's dictum that we live in a world of perfected means and confused ends. With our technological means we can plan our way through the world, we can make life easier, and our welfare states can set up a political technocracy to reduce misery. We can in fact build excellent freeways and residential streets. But unfortunately we do not know where they lead. And one day we put the question of Camus or Sisyphus: What is the meaning or point of all this? What is there in it to make life worth living? Precisely in the outward perfection which still leaves us so inwardly helpless, the unconditioned becomes the theme which sustains us and which might have the rank of reason and goal. But this is the question of lost transcendence.

Once the hidden form of the religious question is perceived, it is found everywhere. In medicine, for example, the problem of the beginning and end of human life has been raised in the debates about abortion and euthanasia. This involves going behind the purely biological quality of life. Similarly penal law is wrestling with the problem of whether punishment should simply prevent damage to the social fabric or whether it has to consider not merely the functional aspect but also the relation between guilt and punishment.

These examples all have the same thrust. They are asking about an unconditioned which cannot be grasped empirically but which still constitutes the ground of our existence. In my view, the real ground is at issue here. For whether we solve this question or fall down on it, whether we decide for this ground or some other, this will change the whole shape of life.

I also believe that the question of the unconditioned which lies behind criticism of the conditioned has been raised with particular vigor by young people today. Alois Schardt impressively drew attention to this some time back when he spoke of some of the collective discoveries of modern youth, for example, that love is more human than war, that there is a human responsibility for the oppressed, or that social systems manipulate the history of individuals. As he saw it, the young think that these things are all against the existing system and they are thus hurling ancient wisdom (without differentiating experiences) against the older generation which should have known and done better.

My point is that behind the criticism of that which conditions and manipulates stands the question of an unconditioned in whose name the criticism is unwittingly made. When drugs seem to bring a state of rapture and relief from all these pressures, when they offer a pseudo-unconditioned—is it so hard to understand why some resort to them? Do we not have here a perversion of the religious question? Is it so surprising that when thousands of young people in America have awakened, rubbing their eyes, from the illusory trip, they have set in motion a Jesus movement, a movement which discloses Jesus to them as a reality and delivers them from the unreality of a dream world? As *Time* succinctly put it, Jesus is for them what their fathers are not.

Is all this simply an uncontrolled ecstatic emotion, a new fad, or can we read in this Jesus movement the clear text of the religious question, which could be expressed only in hidden form in the flight into a utopian world of dope? I will not play the prophet and pretend to have the final answer to this question. I will avoid talking in merely pious terms. But the question is a valid one, and I think I am on good ground when I say that whereas psychotherapy, punishment, and law enforcement cannot solve drug addiction, the figure of Jesus, no matter how fantastically stylized it might be here, does in fact break these fetters. Innumerable young people have thrown off these chains with a cry of liberation.

## 3. Identity

I will now turn to another example which should clarify
the religious question in the background. I have in mind
the identity question which has become so important for
the new generation.

This is the question how I can find myself, my
true I. How can I keep this "I" from being twisted,
diverted, and alienated from itself by external forces
(e.g., social structures and pressures)? I recently read in
a magazine the statement by film star Peter Fonda that
he had lived only five years; before that he was not himself. He, too, was concerned about the identity question.

Perhaps I can illustrate what I mean by a conversation I once had with a man in middle age, which he
began by saying that he had once taken a wrong turn in
life. He ought to have become a musician, he said, in
which case he would have amounted to something. As it
was he took over his father's firm and never came to
himself.

Upset by the sad way he said this, I made a rather
unfortunate reply: "But what do you want? You have
finally made something of it."

"Made something of it? Yes, a house with a gar-
den, a fairly large car and the rest. You are right. I have
made something of it. But I have not made anything of
myself. That's the trouble."

I asked him to be more specific and he replied:
"Do you not see what I mean? A man hears within himself
a voice: This is why you are here. This is what you must
be. This is why you have been put here. And I was made
for music. But look, I have not painted in this sketch of
my life. I have just dabbled a little here and there. So my
life has remained a pretty sorry fragment even though
people admire me as a solid citizen and the press
wrote veritable eulogies about me on the jubilee of the
business."

"If I get your point, what you are saying is that

you are no longer identical with yourself. You have missed your true self."

The answer came like the shot of a pistol: "This is the very phrase I have been looking for. I am not identical with myself."

The conversation went on a good deal longer, but I will break off here. Why have I reported it at all?

Well, I believe that the question of identity—Who am I?—is one that worries all of us. It is a favorite theme of many widely read authors. We find it in the novel by Max Frisch, *Mein Name sei Gantenbein,* and also in his play *Biography: A Game* (E.T. 1969). Both Marx and Sartre say in their different ways that man's identity has been hurt and in some sense warped by social pressures. The structures of society prevent us from achieving congruence with our true being. Instead of being originals, we become copies of our age.

More important, however, than this reference to thinkers and writers is the investigation where this problem of identity becomes an acute one in our own lives. A couple of concluding observations might be made on this.

All of us have often had the impression that the image which others (colleagues, friends, neighbors and so forth) have of us differs sharply from the image we have of ourselves. Often shabby motives are ascribed to us when we are conscious of our own integrity. We thus say: "I am not like that at all. People have a false idea of me." Conversely, when we play a noble and unselfish role for opportunistic reasons, people are often taken in and respect us. Then when we are alone we say: "If they only knew! I am in truth a check that will bounce; I do not have the value put on me." Who am I in reality? Am I what others see in me, or am I what I myself see in me?

I once had an experience which might almost serve as an experiment of thought in this area.

In a family I was visiting the twenty-five-year-old son was present. He was fast becoming a black sheep. He had been mixed up in many unsavory affairs and had

almost broken his mother's heart. Yet suddenly he sat
down at the piano and played some chorales from *St.
Matthew's Passion*. He played these very movingly and
it greatly touched me. His sister, however, angrily whis-
pered in my ear: "What a hypocrite!" She obviously believed that by playing in this way the young man wanted
to make a good impression on me as a theologian.

But was he really a hypocrite? Who and what was
he truly and finally? Was he at the core of his being the
one who was always pilfering from others and pandering
to his weaknesses? Or was he at root the man who played
this chorale and was crying out for deliverance, despising
himself and trying to wash off the filth from his soul?

No man can judge who the other really is. God
alone knows. And possibly his verdict is: This man is
hungering and thirsting after righteousness. He despises
himself. Hence he is dearer to me than many in the white
middle-class west who are so sure of themselves and their
righteousness.

We then think of Dietrich Bonhoeffer. He was
hanged by the Gestapo in the final days of the Second
World War. He had to die because his faith forced him
into confessing resistance against the Nazi regime. His
guards and fellow-prisoners loved him very much because
he did not submit but remained his own man even in
prison. Naturally he knew many hours of despondency.
But he kept this hidden from others.

From this period of imprisonment some poems
have survived and one of these deals with the problem of
identity, that is, with the question: "Who am I?" In it
Bonhoeffer sees the contrast between what others say
about him and what he knows about himself. In their eyes
he comes out of his cell relaxed and cheerful and firm,
while to himself he is disturbed and sick like a bird in a
cage, unable to pray or think or work. Is he what others
think of him or is he what he thinks of himself? Or is he
both at once, a dissembler before men, a pitiable weakling
to himself? Who is he? The question mocks him, but he

finally takes refuge in the fact that whoever he is, God knows him: "I am thine, O God."

What does it mean that God knows me and that I am his?

It means first that we men do not wholly understand either ourselves or our fellows. We do not know either our own identity or that of others. But this need not worry us. Our image is hidden in the heart of God. He knows us.

A second meaning is this. There might be something frightening about the idea that God knows us. That someone knows the last details of our soul, that someone sees us through and through, is a terrifying thought. But if what Jesus has told us about his Father is true, it is no longer frightening but even comforting to be known in this way. For we know that he understands us in love and seeks us in our pain.

To be understood by God, then, is uplifting news. It is what the older vocabulary of Christianity calls gospel. For I am understood here by someone who calls me by name and who is concerned about me. This is what Bonhoeffer has in mind when he says that whoever he is, God knows him and he is God's. There is one who stands by me no matter who I am or what I have done.

My aim has not been to give the answers of the gospel but to deal with our questions about life. And I have been trying to throw light on these questions and to show that behind them is what we call a religious question. Does this not become clear when we raise the question of identity: Who am I?

I will close, then, with a quotation from the Bible which applies this question to each of us personally:

*O Lord, thou hast searched me and known me!*
*Thou knowest when I sit down and when I rise up;*
*thou discernest my thought from afar . . .*
*Thou dost beset me behind and before,*
*and layest thy hand upon me . . .*

*Whither shall I go from thy Spirit?*
*Or whither shall I flee from thy presence?*
*If I ascend to heaven, thou art there!*
*If I make my bed in Sheol, thou art there!*
*If I take the wings of the morning*
*and dwell in the uttermost parts of the sea,*
*even there thy hand shall lead me,*
*and thy right hand shall hold me . . .*
*Search me, O God, and know my heart!*
*Try me and know my thoughts!*
*And see if there be any wicked way in me,*
*and lead me in the way everlasting* (Psalm 139).

# II

# The Question
# of the Church

**Question 1:** *What is your attitude to a democratizing of the church?*

**Answer:** If democratizing of the church means that the initiative in its policy and decisions should not come from the authorities, from above, but rather from below, then I have to be in favor of this. For in this case the political term democratizing simply denotes what in the older vocabulary of the church was more fitly (and more beautifully) described as the principle of universal priesthood. If, however, this way is taken, and everything supports it as I have said, we must be clear about one thing. In our list of priorities the building up of a corresponding awareness, or, better, a corresponding activation of the laity, must take precedence over purely formal and institutional reforms. Structural changes which are not supported by a vital awareness fed on the very substance of the church will remain a sterile law that carries no promise.

When I think of it in this way, I have some serious reservations whether the word democratizing is really the right one. For one thing it is a mistake to import into the church a term taken from outside. When this is done, one slips too easily into the ideologies contained in the word. In this instance the ideology might be that of a general leveling down or we might have an ideologizing of anti-authoritarian emotions and forces of aggression which aim at the destruction not merely of authoritarian structures but of authority as a whole. Indeed the trend towards leveling down can easily carry with it a loss of the ability to distinguish between authoritarian and authority.

Again, recent history has shown that the word democracy has become a shelter or screen for all (I repeat, all) ideologists. It has become a slogan with the help of which they try to make themselves out to be progressive, humanitarian, and concerned for world betterment. Since, then, the concept has become a favorite one in the tactics of concealment and the resultant smoke-screen makes it impossible to know friend from foe, I propose that we should be sparing in our use of this over-burdened term. When coins reach a certain stage of wear and disfigurement they should be taken out of circulation. There are some people who say that the word God has now reached this stage and they thus advocate greater restraint in its use. My friend Paul Tillich often issued similar warnings. Perhaps for the sake of God we should be more careful in using the term God, since too many fingers have handled this coin too. Even great words run the risk of becoming no more than sounding brass and tinkling cymbal. Perhaps the word democratizing, which was once so great but is now so tarnished, belongs to this group. Shortly before this death, Waldemar Besson spoke of "the omnivorous appetite of democratic ideals . . . which are losing all contour and rationality in their obesity" (*Deutsche Zeitung*, 30, p. 21). Why, then, should we import a worn-out cliché when the church has at its disposal its own far better term the "universal priest-hood"?

**Question 2:** *Do you accept the need for a basic alteration in the church's structure?*

**Answer:** Perhaps I should begin by saying that my own linguistic and intellectual taste has to fight a certain aversion when I use the word structure. When the most ignorant adults, and even kindergarten children, can juggle with this word of noble origin, I permit myself the snobbishness of avoiding it as much as possible. In my seminar it is one of the terms I ask my students not to use but to paraphrase. They are good-humored enough to be considerate of their linguistically weaker brother. Face to face with your question, however, I will cut through my scruples, since the material background to which you refer is a very serious one.

Yes, I accept the need for basic structural change in the church. I do so because structures do not have the rank of eternal law laid down by God. They simply have a servant function. They ought to be the best possible organizational arrangement which makes it possible to preach and to act in a new age. On this ground alone they must always be flexible.

But this is not the decisive question. More important is consideration of the criteria and goals according to which their shape should be open to change. My own approach to this is as follows. Before formal matters are regulated, we need to be clear in the name of what causes and contents they are to be regulated. A course in rhetoric and the corresponding rhetorical skill are no good if we do not know what we are going to say with this art of eloquence. Similarly a structural perfecting of the church makes no sense if it does not have the foundation on which alone it can act and speak, if it does not know what it is, what it wants, or what it is saying. So, then, work on the basis of the faith must take precedence over formula regulation. If not, every effort will lead to a futile ticking over, that is, to the terrible formalism of questions of procedure and organization. Who is interested in a church's constitution if the aim which it is meant to serve has been lost to view? A perfectly constituted and organized nothing is a macabre concept. Either the church awakens interest through its message —and naturally this is possible only if it is itself urgently interested in this message and does not instead spin chimeras and wander off into secondary matters—or even as an institution it will excite no interest, and rightly so.

Institutional questions are of genuine concern if what takes place in the institution is alive, if the institution lives by what is central to it, if it is dynamic in essence. But things are very different if it is a dead center which once spilled out glowing lava but no longer does. There is no point in manipulating a corpse. What good is a perfectly organized church, which meets the demand for extreme modernity, if it no longer has anything to say, and those who hear its sermons react with the echo: "I was not there in what the minister said. It may be true, but this truth is irrelevant to me"? In this case, what is done is simply like using cosmetics on a dead person to give the temporary illusion of a living body. It is just as meaningless as when one achieves architectural perfection, constructing sacred buildings according to all the liturgical laws, but no one comes except a few tourists with architectural interests.

Whether a church is living or dead depends exclusively on its proclamation. If someone can show that the church is not a preaching church, and if he can also show that it is not made up of a community which responds to its message in prayer, hymn, and act, then he is describing a corpse.

Your structural question, then, gives me the opportunity to speak to the most sensitive point, as I see it, in the present church crisis. The true problem of the church is not the presence of divided groups within it. This polarization of outlook might well be a sign of living debate which is far better than the undisturbed harmony of a cemetery. No, the problem of the church is its utter failure to recognize the principle of priorities.

What is least of all self-evident is presupposed to be self-evident and incontestable, namely, that we are Christians. Attention is thus unthinkingly focused on the implication of being Christians: human tasks, social changes, problems of joint action, and finally questions of church structure. People rush to the front without even asking about supplies from the stores of spiritual substance. They advance without covering the rear, that is, the message in whose name they are supposed to be acting. The branches are cared for and the root is forgotten. We overlook to our hurt the fact that of the many things we must consider, only one is necessary. Before all of our working and tilling, the pearl of great price must first be secured.

**Question 3:** *In what you have just said, are you not expressing reservations about many church reports and studies?*

**Answer:** Certainly one need only think of the present mania in the church for reports and working papers to find clear signs of its blindness in the matter of priorities. There is merit, of course, in the writings of percipient and informed persons on social and political and economic questions. That these questions have an affinity to theology is incontestable. Having tried to interpret the total reality of the present day theologically in my own *Theological Ethics* (1966 and 1969), I would be the last to deny this. That the church cannot remain silent on abortion or sex is obvious. The difficulty is that so often these statements use only rational arguments which others can also use, or they have a sound ideological criticism but do not show clearly on what basis it is made. To make a truly spiritual utterance we ought to use the particular problems as occasions or pegs for bringing to light the core of the evangelical message and indicating the result when this is left out of account. An illustration might help.

In connection with the very urgent problem of abortion, weak rational arguments and general slogans such as the sacredness of human life can never lead to a solution which is oriented to the gospel. The real need here is to show and establish what human life is: that it is created by God, that it is bought with a price, and that it is inviolable by reason of this alien dignity. This gives rise to the question where the break takes place between purely biological life and this "human" life, that is, where this "human" life begins and ends. The same question arises in the debate about euthanasia. In other words, the real issue is that of the ground of human dignity. It is not enough to keep on repeating the ultimately empty thesis of humanism that life has worth. The futility of this purely conventionally supported thesis may be seen at once from the fact that under the pressure of frustrating circumstances it immediately loses its unconditional character and can be manipulated at will. The unconditional nature of human dignity changes overnight into dependence on many conditions, especially those that are social in character. The position on abortion is a clear sign of this.

We are not saying that our arguments, and especially our theological arguments, do not have to be rational. Of course they do! But we have to remember under what name we are arguing: the name of him who bought us with a price, and who thus sets us under a patronage which makes even unborn and hopelessly sick life sacrosanct and unconditioned. Courage is thus needed to confess the confession on the basis of which we argue.

I am not so remote from the world as to think that one should do this crudely or always blurt it out. But we certainly ought to make it plain whom we are representing. In all that we say as Christians or as the church, reference must be made to that or to him who forces us to speak. The specific cases which demand an open word from us are not ends in themselves, but real opportunities to speak our true and finally saving word. Those who have to speak before many secular panels, as I do, will recognize again and again that this is what is in fact expected of theologians.

If, however, we keep in view the central point in relation to which we speak, the result will be reports which honor this central point and make it an independent theme. But where in fact do we find, in addition to papers on the situation, papers on the matter itself, the real subject? Where do we find, in addition to papers on secular and temporal questions, those that deal with heaven and eternity? Where do we find, except in a few admirable synodical statements, official documents that come to grips with the cross, the resurrection, justification, and grace? Since all these things are related to the incarnation of the Word, there is no reason for concern lest we should become too riveted on heaven and a beyond remote from the present world. To say the Word of God is to say also the world to which it is spoken.

Why then, I ask, are there no papers dealing with these central themes? Do we not have breath enough for them in our hectic preoccupation with the age? Do we fear that we might not be sufficiently agreed on them? Is this why we turn to relevant secular themes in which we can come to easier arrangements?

The church becomes uninteresting if it simply says what others can say just as well and if it is content simply to be another voice in pluralistic group discussions. What the church says on this level is easier when it does not have the Christian packaging. In short, I would be happier with church reports if (a) their themes were made occasions to say what really should be said and (b) what really should be said were a theme itself leading to clarity at home before anything is said abroad.

When the church and its gatherings discuss the general situation or criticize political programs, it seems to me that the priorities are wrong. Christians are simply joining the general chorus of reviewers and critics. Would it not be better and more relevant if they would address themselves to their own problems, for example, religious education, confirmation preparation, and adult Christian education? Are not these very urgent concerns? Is this really the time for excursions into secular topics, no matter how respectable or interesting? If we had had the

courage and self-restraint to turn to these very dangerous and unclarified problems, we could hardly have done
so without also taking into account the broader sphere of
educational planning. Those who introduce the theme of
eternity in one of its dimensions can hardly fail to take
note of the age and its many areas. But stages of urgency
have to be differentiated.

Let me say a final thing on this question. My criticism that the matter of priorities has been forgotten or
wrongly answered, must be applied on both sides. Some
are busy on the periphery and do not notice the loss of
the center. Others go back to the substance of the gospel
and its confession but do not see that this seed of the
gospel is becoming a tree whose branches cover the earth
and therefore demand "publicity." The esoteric quality of
isolated piety is just as alien to the gospel as is the activ-
ism of those who press for immediate change with no
relation to the past. True discipleship demands expression
both at the center and on the periphery. But it stands
under the primacy of the one thing needful.

**Question 4:** *What do you think of pluralism in the
church and the demand for open discussion?*

**Answer:** If pluralism means variety of theological stand-
points and practical emphases, then it can be the sign of
a living organism whose members have different functions. In spite of the variety of functions there can then
be knowledge of the common root and of common fellowship in one body. Without the common center, however,
pluralism can be the mark of centrifugal disintegration.

Before taking up a position in relation to pluralism
one must know what kind of pluralism is at issue. A
church which takes its confession of Jesus Christ seriously
can never become a neutral debating chamber for pet
opinions, even though it must be ready to discuss such
opinions, to listen to them, and to take seriously those who

hold them. Otherwise it could not understand itself as a church which is sent into the world. If it is to go after men who are in the world and are as sheep without a shepherd, it must understand these men, keep track of them, and take to itself their spiritual need. But just because it must call these men out of relativism, indifference, and unbelief, it must never be guilty of relativism, indifference, or unbelief itself.

I know that these things have largely permeated the church today. That they have done so is linked to what I said in answer to the second question. If we accept solidarity with contemporaries without remembering in whose name we do so, this solidarity finally becomes the law of our thinking and action. It becomes an end in itself. Openness to the age then becomes the evil of belonging to it. Love, which forces solidarity on us, always remains aware of why it loves and gives itself to the age. Solidarity for its own sake means bondage to the age and along with this the loss of our own identity. The age becomes our master. In this way the church comes under the threat of centrifugal pluralism. In social, ethical, and political matters it simply says what others say and thus very quickly becomes superfluous. No one has shown this more impressively than the American sociologist P. L. Berger in his excellent book *A Rumor of Angels* (1969).

I should like, then, to rephrase the question a little. It ought to run: What should be the church's attitude to this destructive pluralism in its own ranks?

At issue is the invasion of its task by secularism. Its confession does not cover these tendencies. The church has thus to resist them clearly and uncompromisingly. By the existing constitution synods and leaders are already under obligation to champion and to guard the unfalsified message of the gospel.

How this task will be discharged in detail depends on the specific cases. Church discipline cannot be the only reaction. It can be only the final extreme. A word might be said about this.

We have to remember that even in very abstruse aberrations of thought and action, for example, death of God theology, we usually have not a deliberate rejection of the gospel, but a consequence of it, no matter how erroneous and perverted this consequence might be. The point of departure for most radicals is the desire to proclaim Jesus Christ today and to find new areas for the application of the gospel (e.g., political action). This motive raises the self-critical question whether the gospel is not denied if one will not accept the fact that it does apply to these spheres and is to be actualized in them.

It is true that in the desire for actualization of this kind existing bonds may be snapped and a destructive pluralism introduced. Nevertheless fairness and Christian love demand that the initial motive be taken into account and honored even though one cannot accept what happens in detail. What I mean by honoring of this type is that the church should not put the machinery of bureaucratic resistance in motion against the rise of such phenomena. Instead, it should untiringly seek dialogue, not engaging merely in polemics, but trying with all its might to restore the connection with the common basis of faith. It must even do this with humility, acknowledging that these phenomena point to omissions in its own mission and conduct. Here as always heresies are symptoms that something is missing in the church's proclamation and teaching. They are a scurvy on the body of the church indicating a vitamin deficiency. Hence self-criticism and repentance instead of mere opposition should be the way in which the church reacts to such things. Only along these lines does it have a chance of getting the other side to listen too.

A further point is that in these matters it is never dealing with established fronts but with living men who are also in process of development. Already in extreme representatives of radical movements I think I detect notes one would not have expected some years back. Manifested here, perhaps, are probes after the link with the past. We see in these the power of the Word of God which constantly asserts itself in all our confusion and can intertwine its own history with that of those who expose themselves to it. We should trust this Word and give it time to work. Our churchly self-righteousness might be the very thing that stands in its way.

In sum, we must firmly reject many things and in any case we must draw a clear line. Nevertheless, we should not do this bureaucratically and in no case should bureaucratic reaction be the first step. Instead of separating ourselves from these groups we must talk to them face to face and with the living Word. We must be pastors and not disciplinarians, brothers and not pharisees. Precisely when the church takes responsibility for souls and seeks them, they cannot ignore its opposition. If it does not do this, it remains under obligation to them. What it might put forth as the love that bears, endures, and accepts all things is in truth the sloth of heart which evades responsibility for erring members.

**Question 5:** *Do you think the day of the national church is over?*

**Answer:** I see a form of panic and a lack of faith in the present fixation on the collapse of the national church, the constant talk of its corrosion, and the clearing of the lifeboats as the ship is supposedly going down. The mounting number of departures, understandable and even necessary though some of them may be, is the least impressive reason for defeatism of this kind.

In my view we have not yet fully exploited the possibilities of the national church. We have not done so because we rely on its legal status. We do not have to battle for its daily survival as the members of free churches do, and we get tied up in its routine business.

I do not say this to dampen the desire for freedom. No institution can grant us security against the devil. He can make his way into the free church too. Free churches can become dependent on rich members who finance them or influence them in other ways. Many pastors find to their dismay that they cannot do all they would like to do, for instance, by way of political demonstration, because they would be forced out by influential people and would therefore have to abandon their charges for the sake of conscience. Utopian transfigurations are no more in order here than elsewhere.

In saying that we have not yet exploited all the possibilities of the national church, I am naturally asking that this should be done. As I see it, and have tried to say it, the point of the church is that it should do its basic job. In doing this, and nurturing mature Christians, we shall not merely give new life to the national church. We shall also make the only possible preparation for the contingency that its day is in fact over and congregations will have to stand on their own.


**Question 6:** *Do you see some specific possibilities of urgent action in this field?*

**Answer:** I am glad to have a chance to leave the more general sphere and give a concrete example of what I have in mind.

Basic work means imparting the central contents of the gospel to practicing Christians, marginal members, and those who are completely outside. Before we make a call for faith, we must say what is the object and content of this faith. If we do this properly, a special call for faith will hardly be needed. Ignorance of what the Christian faith is all about is horrendous today. I was talking recently with two students of philology who not only did not know the Lord's Prayer but had never even heard of it. The prime need, then, is for instruction and information.

Even practicing Christians need this, partly because they are confused and partly because they too are ignorant at some points. Studies of what loyal members think about the Lord's supper or the resurrection or the relation of the Genesis stories to theories of evolution can lead to absurd results and false conclusions. But those who are not conversant with the foundations of their faith cannot be mature Christians. They are helpless in face of critical fads or they will take refuge in a narrow conservatism. Congregations consisting of such ignorant people would go down were it not for the external support of the established church. A free church could not be created out of members of this kind.

These considerations have led many people in Hamburg, assistants, young pastors, teachers and students of various faculties, to take part in an information project with me as adviser. A course of adult instruction will be given by me in St. Michael's, Hamburg. Each address will be accompanied by discussions led by members of the project. The leaders of these must be prepared too. In addition to group discussions there will be personal discussions of a pastoral nature for which qualified personnel will be available. This has all been carefully planned over several months. When young men are given an attractive goal they are now as always ready for great effort and self-sacrifice without any payment. This attempt to give information on the faith has struck them as an elementary task which is well worth the time and energy needed. The demand for some self-experience or search for self-identification fades when one is caught up in a great task.

In reporting this venture I hope to encourage others to attempt similar tasks. Either the church will do its basic work and turn to the foundations of its faith or it will die. The local rain of the gospel can easily pass and water more receptive fields. If I read the signs aright, we are close to midnight. Perhaps youth movements will soon engulf us. What are we doing, then, to see to it that young people in their search, and their attraction to utopias, do not remain at a purely ecstatic and emotional level and finally fall victim to an even blacker nihilism? Let us work at the basis so that at the right moment we can say who Jesus Christ is, what he has freed us from, and what he has freed us for.

# III

# The Question of Man

## A. MARXIST MAN

### 1. Authentic and Inauthentic Man

Marxism is in the first instance a doctrine of social relationships. As such it is designed to serve as an intellectual weapon in the battle of the proletariat for liberation. For Marxism this liberation is chiefly economic. Its concern is with the economic exploitation of the working classes and their resultant alienation. Since the basic theme is economic, it might occasion some surprise that we are raising the question of Marxist anthropology. This could give rise to the fear that an alien question is being brought into the system from outside. All the same, the young Marx has a doctrine of man which is not only not concealed but is even set forth programmatically.

#### a. The Place of the Anthropological Question

There are two ways of finding the place of the anthropological question within the basic system.

On the one hand, dialectical materialism says that historical events rest on economic movements and laws. History, then, is strictly and properly economic history. This suggests that man is the product of laws, that is, the effect of economic conditions and not their cause. He cannot be their cause since they follow the law of dialectic and are outside the sphere of freedom when this is understood as the possibility of intervention. From this angle

man seems to play only a small secondary part. He is just
the appendage of movements which work themselves out
on him as on an object.

On the other hand, there is a very different way
of integrating anthropology into the Marxist system. A
Roman Catholic expositor of Marxism, Theodor Stein-
büchel, can say: "If Christianity is concerned about man,
so too is Marx." What he means is that man is the primary concern of both. It is because of man that they are
polemically interested in one another. If Marxism were
simply economic theory, it is hard to see why Christianity
and Marxism should be in such passionate controversy.
For Christianity has no specific economic theory. Indeed,
as many religious Socialists have pointed out, it is wholly
compatible with Marxist economic theory.

That anthropological interest is central in Marxist
thought, at any rate in the younger Marx, is apparent at
once without express citations. Schoeps (*Was ist der
Mensch?* 1960, p. 33) rightly says that the younger Marx
has much in common with Kierkegaard. He, too, is concerned about inauthentic and alienated man on the one
side and authentic man on the other, although he defines
the relation between them differently. In his criticism of
Hegel's philosophy of religion (Kröner, Vol. 209, p. 216),
Marx says that theory can grasp the masses once it dem-
onstrates *ad hominem,* and it does this when it becomes
radical. To be radical is to get to the root of things. In
man's case the root is man himself.

### b. *Man as the Chief Theme*

Does it need to be proved further that man is in fact
the real theme, not just for theory but for the program of the battle? The only possible practical liberation
of Germany is liberation from the standpoint of the
theory which declares man to be the supreme being
(Kröner, p. 223). Theoretically expressed, then, the goal
of the battle—and this again is an anthropological thesis
—is the true resolution of conflict between existence and

essence, between objectification and self-activity, between freedom and necessity, between individual and species. He, authentic man who is no longer alienated but has come to himself, is the solved puzzle of history and he knows that he is the solution (p. 235). On this basis one has to say that man is the true theme of Marxist thought, not man in himself but man in relation to the material conditions of his existence which decide whether he remains enslaved in alienation or seizes the social opportunity to win through to authenticity.

It is important to look at the specific occasion which gave rise to Marxism, namely, the situation of the working classes in the epoch of early capitalism. The Marxist ethos developed in a passionate movement of resistance to two symptoms of the sickness of modern society which are closely interrelated. The first is the new form of slavery in which a certain portion of humanity is devalued into an impersonal mass which has the rank of a mere machine. The second is the reduction of man to a means to an end, the end being viewed as the profit of a small parasitic class. The initial fervor of Marxist movements is thus to be found in their protest against dehumanizing. In this sense one might say that they have a humanitarian beginning.

If, then, we are right in ascribing an important role to the anthropological starting-point in the Marxist system, we have to ask at once the question how and in what sense man arises for Marx. Our next discussion will try to answer this question. It will contain a sharp theological questioning of Marx.

### c. Economic Man

In Marx, man appears as an object of social pity and the resultant social therapy. What is at issue is how man can free himself from his alienation and deprivation face to face with a wrong social system. Man is not—this is an additional negative thesis—an object of independent interest devoted to the mystery of his existence or nature even where this transcends his economic relation. Man is viewed only in his relation to social and economic factors. He can be changed and brought to himself only by changing this dominating element. In the last analysis, then, he is simply an exponent and function of this particular complex of reality.

Marx thinks that he has said all that needs to be said about man when he describes him as economic man. The economic dimension is not just one dimension of human life among others, even if a most vital one. Man's whole existence is seen as an emanation of this particular element. The partial is made the whole. Theologically, then, Marxist thought has the character of a heresy. For heresy arises when one aspect of doctrine is made the whole and elephantiasis sets in. Marx is an anthropological heretic inasmuch as he reduces the whole of existence to one sector. We may thus expect, and will in fact find, that Marx, notwithstanding his central interest in man, misses the essence of humanity and that in his thinking the image of man is a spectral one that escapes our grasp.

But let us go now to the heart of the matter and look at this anthropology on its negative side where Marx speaks of man's dehumanizing and alienation. What does this mean? We can find out from his interpretation of capitalism.

### d. The Concept of Alienation

We come to the loss of humanity, to man's degradation to a material working force, when we study what Marx calls the theory of surplus value. The worker does not receive the due return on his work but only enough for minimal existence. He is thus no more than a dynamic and impersonal agent of his working power and is not valued as a person, since a person is more than the productivity which nature has invested in it. The pseudo-humanity of capitalism, which is represented by the surplus value theory, might be summed up as follows: The worker is not loved, but he cannot be allowed to go hungry since his power to work must be maintained.

This is utterly non-human, since the worker is no longer treated as an end in himself but only as the means to an end, that is, the meeting of a given production quota. Immanuel Kant found the epitome of the non-moral in the evaluating of man as the means to an end instead of an end in himself. This treating of man as a thing comes to expression already in the idea of the working force. For this equates the worker with natural forces like steam or electricity. Since the worker has to sell this force, but he himself is also identical with this force, the result is that he is constrained to sell himself.

The slavery which arises in this way leads to man's alienation from himself. This comes to manifestation in two forms.

The first is social and economic. Man undergoes deformation by coming under the domination and control of his products. He is no longer the subject of his products and their production; he is their victim and slave. Since one group, the capitalist class, governs the work of others and uses them simply as a means to the end of profit, that is, as human material, humanity is divided into consumers and victims. Man becomes a mere object and bearer of a function; this is his extreme self-alienation.

The classes are the social and institutional representation of this self-alienation. Thus the basis of self-alienation is the division of work whereby some must work for others and workers have no control over their products. The worker is thus reduced to his function. A depraved soul corresponds to this degrading function (Kröner, p. 516).

The second form of self-alienation is in religion and ideology. The ruling class in every age forms ideologies to justify its monopoly, to secure itself, and to throw dust in the eyes of others, so that they will not see their self-alienation as such and therefore will not protest against it. As Marx sees it, religion too is one of these ideologies. Religion intensifies and perpetuates alienation by offering a substitute consolation whereby man mixes up his real relations, finds comfort by hoping for a better life hereafter, and accepts the misery of this world as the supposed will of God. He is thus prevented from desiring or achieving a real change in his situation.

This is the true impulse behind Marxist atheism. Religion does not rescue man from his self-alienation but holds him fast in it. This makes it clear that in Marxism in its original form we may see features of positive humanism. Marx seems to be truly concerned about man, even about his personality.

## 2. The Break in Marxist Anthropology

Can Marxism sustain its humanitarian beginning? This is an urgent question since everywhere we seem to see the opposite. The very fact that Marxism has established itself in the form of political dictatorship teaches us that humanity has obviously suffered a serious personal loss, that in some forms of outworking at least the dignity and freedom of man have not been respected as one might have expected from the early stages, and that here we come up against the same mechanization and emptying of soul under another sign. (We in the west obviously cannot throw stones in this regard, since we live in glass houses too, if for different reasons.)

Even if we cannot concede that Marxist-Leninism is a consistent development of Marxist anthropology, but perceive a profound structural change, this does not release us from the task of posing our critical question but, in fact, makes it all the more urgent. Indeed, the question itself is sharpened. It must now run: How has it come about that Marxist-Leninism has arisen out of the original Marxist ideology and can obviously feel justified in appealing to it?

Our core problem, then, is this: How has there taken place in Marxism this break which threatens to lead away from the humanitarian beginning to inhumanity? Do we have here an inconsistency, a decline, an abandonment of the original ideal? Are we dealing here with the very essence of Marxism or with a perversion of its essence?

This question is a highly important one. On the answer to it depends the attitude of the church of Jesus Christ to Marxism. Is the church to reject Marxism or can it see in it correctives which show that it is still open to true humanity? Can it be that the combination with atheistic anthropology is not unconditionally constitutive for Marxism, but as a scientific sociology it can be just as open or closed to Christianity as natural science? As Christian observers we must also scrutinize ourselves at this point, since it might be that in ourselves, as Marxists see only too well, Christian and middle-class elements have fused and distort our vision. At any rate we must keep before us this possible source of error.

### a. The Idealistic Origin

Perhaps we can answer our cardinal question better if we consider the second strand in the rise of Marxism. (The first has to do with abuses in the capitalist order.) We are referring to the intellectual origin, that is, to the way that Marxism arose out of Hegelian philosophy. In this regard we must especially ask how far Marxism with its extreme materialism is not guilty of an Oedipus complex in relation to its idealistic parentage.

Hegel's basic thought was that all world occurrence is a self-development of the spirit. The spirit does not exist abstractly in itself apart from the world. It exists in its unfolding. The world spirit gradually moves up from the stage of unconscious nature to the stage of awakening consciousness of itself. This consciousness is to be found in human thought and this thought for its part has a rich range of possibilities of development from the phase of mere awakening to that of lofty reflection. The final stage arrives when man raises the whole content of the divine spirit to the level of clear philosophical knowledge. In this sense Hegel viewed himself as the ultimate coming of the spirit to consciousness.

The essential point in the Idealist-Marxist debate is this. In Hegel, spirit is not something which is, to put it crudely, produced by the thought or brain of man, as though man were at the beginning of all spiritual movements. The exact opposite is the case. Thinking man is last. First is the world spirit itself which knows the various stages of its development. It takes shape first in the cosmos in organic and inorganic nature. Nature clearly bears its traces, for it is cosmos, a meaningful construct which in its causal and final subjection to law bears witness to spirit.

Nature, however, is only an object of the developing spirit in the stage of its self-alienation. It cannot respond to it with consciousness. Only in the human spirit, at a later stage of development, does the absolute spirit become conscious of itself, so that it can engage in self-reflection. Therefore, when man thinks, it is not strictly he who thinks but the absolute spirit itself that thinks through him. The principle thus arises: The absolute spirit thinks in the finite spirit and the finite spirit knows itself as the absolute spirit.

### b. *Man as a Transitional Stage in Intellectual Processes*

In relation to our understanding of Marxism it is important to note that in Hegel's idealistic system man himself plays a relatively secondary role. He is simply a transitional stage in higher intellectual processes, as later he will be for Marx a transitional stage in economic processes. Related to this is the fact that Hegel can find no true place for the individual. Human history as the self-actualization of the spirit knows the individual only as an inauthentic bearer or transitional point. As an individual he is inferior to the species, which is general and is thus closer to the idea. One can even say that as the species brings itself forth in general, and as this bringing forth takes place in the flow of generations, the species constantly reduces the individual to a mere transition and thus far slays and uses it.

The sexual absorption of the individual into the species so that the species may maintain itself as a supra-individual entity is the first step toward the removal of true individuality, that is, toward death. Hegel is expressing this strange union of love and death when he says that the species sustains itself only by the perishing of individuals, which fulfil their destiny in the processes of mating and, having no higher destiny, go down to death (*Enzyklopädie* §370, p. 327, Meiner). One might almost say that the original incongruity of the individual and the general is the original sickness and the native seed of death (§375, p. 331).

In the present context Hegel is important in two ways. We can now see more precisely why we had to say earlier that the individual man is not the one who produces but a comparatively insignificant transitional stage of the spirit which uses him to achieve its own purposes and to achieve consciousness of itelf. This being so, the role of historically important individuals in Hegel is also clear. They do not have any initiative in the historical process, as spectators might think. They are used instrumentally by the cunning of reason. No matter how Marxism rebelled against its idealistic parent, it unmistakably inherited one factor from this parent, namely, the secondary role of the individual who is caught up in the flow of supra-individual processes.

### c. The Break with Hegel

We are now in a position to consider the point at which Marxism arises from the standpoint of intellectual history. This is the point at which it breaks with the Hegelian tradition. It has now become sufficiently clear that one cannot understand the decisive tendencies in Marxism if one does not take into account its genesis in idealism and see how this is still at work even in its negation. One can understand the atheistic and anti-Christian thrust of Marxism only if one realizes to what extent Marxism came into conflict with its true origin.

The younger or left-wing Hegelians, from whom Marx emerged, felt that they had to put an urgent question which is suggested even by Hegel himself, namely, whether his way of relating the world spirit and the human spirit should not be reversed. Is it true, this school asked, that there exists any absolute spirit at all which uses human consciousness to become conscious of itself? Is this not an illusion in the sense that the absolute spirit is simply a projection of the human spirit? If so, the absolute spirit is just our own alter ego which we perceive only by an optical illusion, namely, a secret act of objectification.

In saying this we have already described the decisive reaction to Hegel. Feuerbach, working out the inversion in the concept of God, says along these lines that the principle of his philosophy does not lie in Spinoza's substance, nor in Kant's intelligible I, nor in Hegel's absolute spirit, nor in any entity of this kind which is abstracted from true reality, but in the most real of all real beings, in what is in truth the most real being, man himself. Man thinks the spirit; the spirit does not think man. This most real being for Feuerbach is not, of course, the individual man but man as a species, a type. At this point one may still detect Hegel's aversion to what is individual.

#### d. The Extreme Counterposition

This is not the place to examine all the varieties of left-wing Hegelianism. But the extreme form of this demands closer inspection. This is developed in almost grotesque fashion when Max Stirner in his famous book *Der Einzige und sein Eigentum* (1845) makes individual man the representative of the last and in fact the only reality. What he has in mind is the man who is freed from all that cannot be shown to be real, that is, from commitment to metaphysical, logical, ethical, and legal norms, who stands before us and enjoys his "moment" simply as a physical entity that is to be measured by size and weight. For him there can in truth be no more than a discontinuous moment. For if he were to refer to the future, which would be to imply temporal continuity, he would have to presuppose norms, values, and goals for himself.

In other words, the most real being is not individual man with his intellectual existence but individual man as a natural animal independent of his intellectual existence. According to this logic, man is thus reduced and shriveled up to the physical part of his ego. Once this man begins to think, he is again in the unreal world of fantasy which may be seen in philosophy, religion, and ethics.

Finally, then, the individual is the only thing that is real. For with ideal norms every possibility of communication with other men is also scrapped, since this communication can take place only in the sphere of relations which transcend individual specimens of humanity and are to that extent ideal. It cannot even be said that man is a species, since this implies the communication of individuals too. The only form of contact, then, is the unrelated proximity of physical bodies. Here Hegel's doctrine of the absolute spirit is changed into a nihilistic, anarchistic, and atheistic anthropology which rules out any further development, and even the concept of anthropology itself, for the simple reason that here human thought enters the sphere of the irrational, the alogical, the silence of reason. For once reason begins to speak, illusion again engulfs us.

### e. The Reversal to Marxism

It is necessary to pursue the reversal of Hegelism idealism to the extreme limit at which it changes into the completely materialistic solipsism of Max Stirner. It is necessary to consider for a moment the complete desolation of this world without spirit or morality in which the stillness of night reigns and man is left alone in the darkness of a lunar landscape. Only thus can one grasp how absolute and terrible is the end of idealism. Only thus can one fix the point in intellectual history where the reversal into Marxist philosophy takes place and might almost be described as necessary.

Marx and Engels followed up the logic of Stirner's position. Thus Engels, writing to Marx in 1844, speaks of the noble Stirner, noble because he is bound to make a profound impression if there is the courage to draw the final deductions from his thought. His egoism, says Engels, is pushed to such a point, is so wild and yet so deliberate, that he cannot remain for a moment in this onesidedness of his, but is bound to make a change to communism (Marx-Engels, *Ausgabe*, III, 1, p. 7).

This passage is particularly important because it fixes so precisely the point at which Marxism makes its entry into intellectual history. It is also important to see how the law of Hegel's historical dialectic works itself out here. Max Stirner with his materialistic individualism is the antithesis of Hegel's thesis regarding the spirit and the absorption of the individual. We have already seen this. The question of the further development of the antithesis is now the issue. Two possibilities seem to exist, resulting from the placing of the accent in the phrase "materialistic individualism."

In the first instance, when the accent is placed on "materialistic," the reaction will be to a new variation of idealism. We need not pursue this here, although revived forms of idealism are strong in some types of revisionary socialism. When the accent falls on "individualism," however, the corresponding antithesis is communism. This is the possibility which is followed up in Marxism. At the same time another factor becomes significant here which helps us to understand the Hegelian origin of Marxism. In this reversal into Marxism the materialistic basis is transcended in the Hegelian sense of not just being negated or overcome but also kept in modified form.

Two things make this plain. The first is the way in which man is set in relation to material economic laws which determine his existence. The second is the way in which the spiritual sector is understood. In what follows we shall deal with the first of these, namely, the significance of economic processes.

### 3. Insight into Necessity as the Basis of Human Action

The way in which man is regarded in Marxism as a function of the historical substructure reminds us of man's dependence on natural laws. This is particularly plain in the interpretation of revolution as Marx illustrates this with his image of the shift from quantity to quality. In the course of social change (that is, the quantitative increase of property on the one side and its decrease on the other, followed by an increasing quantitative perversion of the relation between the narrowing class of owners on the one side and the gigantically expanding host of dispossessed workers on the other), there necessarily arise nodal points where the quantitative changes into the qualitative. When this happens the nodal point of revolution arrives.

In revolution, one might think, the freedom of man breaks forth. Revolution is an event of human spontaneity accompanied by emotions. In it man breaks with the sloth of the past. He no longer sees himself as simply the effect of historical conditions, for example, the social orders. In free spontaneity he breaks his chains and declares himself to be the creator of new conditions. At the same time we have seen that revolution as this specific phenomenon of human freedom is still subject to the necessity of natural law, and has the quality of a physical nodal point. But does not this take away man's being as a subject and remove altogether all that is human? (In this respect revolution simply serves as a model.) To press the question: Can there be in this complex the representatively human situation of responsibility?

### a. The Problem of Responsibility

To follow up this concept, responsibility can arise only when two conditions are met. First, I must act freely and stand by what I do. If I act in a trance or at gun point I cannot be held responsible by men. Second, in what I do I must be responding to the claim of a higher authority, for example, that of truth. Responsibility means being under the necessity of making a response, of giving an answer.

In principle, then, responsibility is not possible when there is no confrontation with an entity to which I must answer and which is thus independent of me. In principle it is not possible when all that I think and do is part of a dialectically conditioned process in which my personal ego has no place and my impersonally conceived ego is simply used. If freedom is still spoken of in this connection (and what philosophical system has ever extinguished it?) then it can no longer be the sign of voluntary spontaneity but can only signify insight into historical necessity. We must look at this concept of freedom for a moment.

Wolfgang Leonhard, in his well-known book *Die Revolution entlässt ihre Kinder,* tells us of the strange impression which proclamations of freedom in the western press made on the young functionaries of Bolshevik high schools. For us, he says, freedom was insight into historical necessity. Since we were the only ones who on the basis of scientific theories had this insight, we were free, whereas those in the west who did not have these theories, who were thus ignorant and helpless in face of historical development, and who were even playthings of it (in spite of their proclamations of freedom), were not free.

In other words, the west takes freedom to mean

that one can do what one likes. It does not even suspect that historical forces are controlling this supposed freedom and thus making it an illusion. The seriousness of this challenge should not be overlooked. To reply by stating in confessional fashion that we represent the free way of life in the west is empty rhetoric. It frightens me when I hear again and again these empty phrases. They are the signs of an immobilizing security which is not merely out of place but positively dangerous when we are on the edge of the abyss. A serious effort of thought is demanded at this juncture.

### b. *The Rule of Necessity*

What does it mean to say that freedom is insight into necessity? Dialectical materialism champions the thesis that in neither nature nor society does anything happen by chance. Necessity rules. Hence everything that is at work in history and the sphere of human action is guided by objective laws. They have the same force as the laws of nature. Now communism views itself as a movement of liberation. It seeks to change the world and not just to interpret it. Hence it comes up against the problem of freedom at a basic level. For the desire to change the world logically presupposes the freedom to be able to do so.

In this framework the answer to the question of the relation between freedom and necessity can take only the form proposed in the famous definition given by Engels. Freedom does not lie, he says, in an imagined independence of natural laws but in the knowledge of these laws and in the possibility which this knowledge gives to let them work in a planned way for specific goals. Freedom is not active interference with the laws—this is impossible—but collaboration with them according to plan. This collaboration naturally presupposes knowledge. This knowledge is to be understood as knowledge of the rules of movement of the material and economic substructure of history.

Historical freedom as mere insight into necessity is then followed by the eschatological freedom of fulfilling history. This second form of freedom—the eschatological —brings about what Marxist Leninism calls the leap into the sphere of freedom. For when society takes charge of the means of production, the dominion of the product over those who produce it ends. With it also ends the necessity of the previous course of history and its authority over man. The objective alien forces which have hitherto ruled history come under man's control. They thus allow him to be a subject again. Only this eschatological stage of history brings man's final emancipation from the animal kingdom, allows him to be entirely on his own, and thus offers him the chance of unbroken humanity.

Students of Hegel will easily detect here the materialization of his doctrine of spirit. Developing into subjective spirit, man becomes free and sees in all reality a manifestation of the same spirit which comes to consciousness of itself in him as finite spirit. In thus recognizing his identity with that which works through everything objective, he is absolutely free. Being free and not being determined by anything alien are one and the same thing. I am free when I am on my own (*Philosophie der Geschichte, Philos. Bibl.*, p. 32). I am free when I will what is willed by the world spirit and when, therefore, what is willed is no longer a decree for me. As history is a step into awareness of this identity, world history is also a step into awareness of freedom (p. 40). The eschatological sphere of freedom is thus a sphere of perfected humanity in the sense of man's being on his own.

### c. The Dynamic Thrust of History

Following Hegel, the Marxist sees an ascent to freedom by a recognition of the anonymous forces to which the middle class is blinded and the harmonizing of a knowledge of their historical course with his program of action. As a result he is not worn out any more, as Kantian dualism between freedom and necessity demands, by conflict with the ineluctabilities of history, for example, economic trends, the laws of mass psychology, and many other factors of the supra-individual historical sphere. Instead, he uses the thrust of history, harnesses all its waters to his mills, and powers his own history-changing dynamic by the forces of history itself. As a result he acts in sympathy with history instead of in antipathy against it.

Here, in distinction from Hegel, an "economical" consideration can be seen at work. It is more exhausting to resist the flow of history and more economical to power one's own will by falling in line with its thrust. The economic is the method as well as the object of Marxist thought. The object is first grasped in thought and then worked on in action.

We can understand the great attraction that this view and program exert. Its attraction does not rest on its materialistic background, which evokes polemical questioning, but on the fact that freedom is not merely proclaimed here as an ideal wish but is exposed to the pressure of reflection. This reflection discovers certain controlling forces in history. Only in relation to these can freedom come to itself if it is not to be blind, if it is to be more than an empty phrase. To say freedom without any knowledge of the necessity to which it must adapt itself is to say nothing.

In Communist eyes, then, the free west is not willing anything different from its eastern opponent when it says "freedom." The difference is in thought. To will freedom as distinct from terror or ideological tyranny can only mean having different ideas of freedom. Freedom has to be grounded; otherwise it has no ground. Ground is deliberately used here both as a logical category and also in the sense of a real life-foundation. Marxist Leninism, then, contains a deep question which cannot be answered by declamation but only by argument. The problem of answering this question seems to be the great task for adult westerners at the level both of thought and of decision.

### d. *The Reason for the Reduction of Man*

At this point we come up once more against the reduction of the personal sphere in Marxism. For the question has to be faced: Is not freedom restricted on this view to the ability to give an insight, that is, the insight into historical necessity? But what would move man to claim this insight? What empowers him to do so?

As regards the proletariat, one might answer that the compulsion is that of the social misery which is to be overcome and from which means of liberation are to be sought. Along these lines the first need is to track the course of the historical process so as to be able to move with it and therefore to act productively instead of unsuccessfully opposing it. In this case insight into necessity is simply the product of economic pressure. It is not at all what has previously been regarded as freedom, that is, the ability to stay clear of all pressure, to assert oneself in face of laws, and, for example, to achieve a triumph of the freedom of the spirit over the sufferings of the body.

If, however, instead of thinking of the workers, we think of men like Marx himself, the actual men who set forth the theory of history and proclaim their insights into necessity, this explanation will not do. These philosophers of Marxism, thinkers like Marx and Engels, are not under the pressure of the fate of the proletariat. What is it, then, that forces them to claim this freedom? Is it pity for the alienated humanity of the workers? If so, then the next question arises at once: What is the source of this pity? What is the worth of these men which makes this intellectual sacrifice worthwhile? To this question we have no answer.

If I am right, freedom and empowering for it only arise either as measures of self-help under economic pressure or as acts on behalf of man whose nature and worth are obscure. But should it not be shown and said what man is in order to explain on what ground he should be helped, for example, out of love? In the New Testament love is grounded on the nature of man. He is the being about whom God is concerned and whom he has bought with a price. Because God is concerned about him, we must be concerned about him too.

### e. The Exclusion of the Personal Sphere

The personal sphere is thus excluded and unillumined. The final thing to be said about man is simply that in his being and consciousness he is controlled by the economic substructure, the class situation, and that he is the agent of this situation. All his impulses and decisions flow out of this situation. They are just reactions to it and cannot be traced back to convictions which have their own origin in the moral ego or conscience.

How are we to understand this? The answer is that when decisions and convictions arise they take form in the consciousness. But this is simply a reflection of the economic basis and is functionally dependent on it. Dominant thoughts are simply an ideal expression of dominant material relations grasped as thoughts. The relations which make a class dominant are therefore thoughts of domination (Marx, *Deutsche Ideologie*, Kröner, pp. 373f.).

Now it must be said that this diagnosis of Marx has in many respects the force of a corrective. It shows how little basis there is for the idea that philosophy comes down from heaven to earth with no presuppositions and how important it is to make it clear that the social situation does in fact influence our consciousness and our decisions. Nevertheless, as Schoeps says in his *Was ist Mensch?* (p. 53), it is only simplistically that man believes he has found the one absolute principle which explains complex modes of human behavior and with which the laws of historical development can be determined and predetermined. To think that human behavior can be read on the sleeve is sheer stupidity. In face of the truly great phenomenon of world history, no explanatory principle can suffice, not even the materialistic. Even so ephemeral an event of the recent past as the Hitler movement cannot be seriously explained in this way. Thus, as Schoeps concludes, the actual course of history continually falsifies Marxist interpretations and prognoses, even though they sound realistic because they are harmonized with the demands of economic reason. Why is this? Because Marxists have a false anthropology, because Marx has forced a reduction on man with his thesis of an exclusive basis of human consciousness.

## 4. The Degradation of Man as a Mere Function

The exclusion of personality and the reduction of man to the status of a mere function of the substructure are the ultimate reasons why we constantly come up against impersonality in the various forms of communism. This is why we find only collective thought and action, why vocabulary and ideas are schematized, why there is a liking for the clichés of propaganda, why there can be no place for range and variety in intellectual structures, for swimming against the stream, for not howling with the pack.

### a. Marxist Criticism of Marxism

A sign of how strongly the dangerous possibilities of development are seen within socialism itself may be found in the so-called revisionist movements. To be sure, the revisions do not amount to more than postulates. They have little chance of bringing about the desired corrections or even penetrating into Marxist thought at all. We shall mention here only two revisionist postulates which are especially important in the present context. As the leading revisionists E. Bernstein and L. Woltmann put it, social science cannot be pursued in the same way as natural science. Sociological laws cannot be formulated in the same way as natural laws. There can be no exact prediction of coming developments with the help of such laws.

Predictions will not come true and have not done so. For example, the plight of the working classes has not worsened. By self-help (strikes) and other social measures (unions), that is, by human initiative, which is not determined by any natural law, there has been a steady improvement of conditions for both workers and the middle class. In other words, exact prognoses cannot be fulfilled because they do not take into account the intervention of the national and purposeful will. For this reason, however, ethical and ideal values have to be taken seriously and cannot be regarded as purely functional ideologies. Religion, art, and law influence economic relations, just as economic conditions influence the religious or artistic superstructure.

In the face of these Marxist proposals for revision, one must put in all earnestness the question of how far they reject the true position of Marxism, if they are intent on not just revising it but negating it (although naturally this does not mean that some of its economic theories and insights might not be accepted).

We cannot go into that question here. I have mentioned revisionism only to show that fear of the dominant impersonality of Marxism does not have its origin in theological prejudices but is felt even within Marxism itself. Just as early Marxism intervened in favor of the human when it opposed capitalist society, so revisionism is intervening in favor of the human when this time it opposes Marxism itself.

An impressive reference to the threat of impersonality may also be seen in the atheistic meditation on prayer in the book by M. Machovec, *Vom Sinn des menschlichen Lebens*. Whereas modern man lives in virtue of a permanent forgetting of the I, an inner dialogue used to be assured by religion. In prayer man did not really speak with God, as he thought, but with his ideal self.

But he achieved an inner dialogue which enabled him to control life and not lose his I in external things. Modern man, by banishing prayer without demystifying and liberating the human element in it, has lost the inner dialogue, and can no longer objectify or overcome the sense of his own weakness or guilt, that is, the failures of the empirical I. Necessarily, then, he suffers inner impoverishment. The sovereign ruler of things who forgets his I loses the most precious of all things, communication with human inwardness. As regards inner dialogue, the medieval monk with his meditations was really more advanced than modern man.

Machovec is obviously on the horns of a dilemma. On the one side he accepts the Marxist criticism of religion with an obviously rationalistic accent. On the other hand he sees that the Marxist emancipation from theology poses a threat to anthropology. The basic role of things robs the human of its autonomy and threatens the freedom of man's inner being. The human is left defenseless against the material world outside. Prayer is asked for, then, as an exercise in humanity, although it has to be demythologized. What must be kept is simply its creative function in the sphere of the human, not its original purpose as talking with God, which did incidentally fulfil the human function too.

Here if anywhere, in this book by a modern Marxist, where the latent question of the reality of the human breaks forth again, we can see the hidden question of God.

### b. Communist Humanism

This brings us to the deepest break that takes place in communism. It consists in the fact that the remarkable contradiction between its personal concern on the one side and its economic and materialistic depersonalizing on the other has in both theory and practice increasingly been settled in favor of the latter. But did not Marxist Leninism retain the slogan of positive humanism? Did not

even Stalin, to quote a particularly extreme and ambivalent figure, use this concept too?

A speech of Stalin quoted by Fritz Lieb (*Russland
unterwegs* [1945], pp. 262ff.) is extraordinarily instruc-
tive in interpretation of the slogan "positive humanism."
In it he argues emotionally against greater concern for a
runaway mare than a missing worker. He then adds that
earlier in the days of the revolution the stress had to be
on the promotion of technology, but now one must turn
to the man who masters it. This human interest is demanded by the sign of technology itself. (It should be
noted that technology rather than a categorical imperative or a command of God lays the emphasis on the
human.) Every capable and trained functionary must be
cared for and his development fostered. Men must be
carefully cultivated, properly organized in the process of
production, and provided with better qualifications if
a great army of cadres is to be raised up for technical
production.

### c. Utility as a Standard

Since this is not a solitary argument but the usual one,
it can be regarded as representative and may be interpreted accordingly. Thus the new accent on man, and
the positive humanism corresponding to it, do not rest
on the belief that man stands over against the mechanical
and instrumental world, that he is the bearer of personal
worth, or of the infinite value of the human soul, or of
divine likeness. The point is that in the hierarchy of
technical means man is exalted and given a head position
as the one who controls machines. He is the functionary
in a world of functions. This is his nobility. His utility,
not his worth, is what counts. Pragmatism rules.

The question which has to be put to this form of
humanism is, therefore, as follows. Does it not resemble
its original capitalist opponent in the fact that it regards
man as the means to an end, measuring his importance
by his role in the process of production? This means-to-

an-end position can be detected when we put the extreme question (extremes are a good place to find the truth!) whether man is simply the bearer of a material dignity and function, whether he has importance, for example, in terms of the economic value he represents, or whether, apart from this value, he is sacred even when he becomes older, weaker, and less useful. The latter is truly human in our view.

If, however, man is important only as the bearer of material value, the highest evaluation put on him, perhaps expressed in awards, social privileges, and higher salaries, should not be confused with respect for him as a person. How little this kind of respect is really at issue is clear from the fact that this whole approach carries with it the possibility of liquidating those who have out-lived their usefulness.

### d. Exclusion of Basic Anthropological Questions

It is a fact that the question of the nature of man is not raised apart from the pragmatic aspect. Another test case arises here. Twice the question of man seems to come up. The first is when Marx speaks of alienation. Can he speak of alienation without measuring it by a norm of what man is in himself, in his nature, positively?

Strange as it may seem, this is not impossible. We ourselves can often say what is inhuman. But difficulty arises when we have to say, positively, what is human. To know the bad is not to imply knowledge of the good. In order to know what man or the good is, one's source of information must be disclosed. For example, is man the image of God or simply a functionary in the economic process? In negations, however, in the description of what is inhuman, one does not have to make the same disclosure. A massive mistreatment of man, for example, his cynical exploitation, runs contrary to both views of man.

Since, however, we usually speak only of man in general, the concept has become weak and unworthy of

credit and it amounts to little more than prattle. When
we speak of man we mostly have in mind only a cipher for
the opposite of the inhuman, that is, a negation of the
negation. Merely from the fact, then, that Marx knows
the concept of alienation and inhumanity, we cannot conclude that he also knows the positive side, the actual
nature of man.

Does this mean that Marx is acquainted with radical evil in the form of alienation? There are good grounds
for questioning this. Leszek Kolakowski, in his book *Der
Mensch ohne Alternative* (1961), is surely right when he
points out that the question of radical evil cannot arise
here since man does not stand before radical decisions
concerning absolute good and evil but only before values
limited and relativized by historical processes. Good and
evil come to light only in personal and unconditional
conviction. Only individual men and their acts come
under moral assessment. For there can be no moral
assessment when no attention is paid to purposes. But
purposes are a matter for individual men. Consequently
it is impossible to pass moral judgment on an anonymous
historical process and its success or failure (pp. 106ff.).

### e. Socialization as a Free Act

A second control is also possible for our test case. Marx
on occasion could speak positively of the nature of man,
of authentic man, that is, when he depicted this man as
freed from alienation and brought to himself. He did
this in his eschatology. It is set under the slogan of the
leap into freedom. This leap takes place when society
takes over the means of production and the rule of the
product over the producer is ended. This also ends the
battle for individual being. Only then does man finally
leave the animal world and achieve genuinely human conditions. The socialization previously thrust on him by nature and history now becomes his own act. This is the
leap of humanity out of the kingdom of necessity into the

kingdom of freedom (*Handbuch des Weltkommunismus* § 23).

Man in himself, authentic man, is no longer here an object of relations. He achieves socialization by his own free act. But here again do we not have a negative statement, a negation of the negation? Are we not simply told that man is no longer alienated without being told, as we might have been according to the anthropological starting-point, what man is positively? How will history continue? Will it continue at all? There are no longer any hostile forces with which to contend, whether in society (for classes have vanished) or in the human soul. Is the man of the last days good, perfect, without evil? All this remains obscure. A man like Robert Havemann entertains utopian ideas on the subject. But the fact that he raises the theme seems to confirm the instinct of the chief ideologists that it is an alien body in the system.

### f. The Vague Picture of Man

There seems to be in Marx only one hint as to the nature of man (cf. *Deutsche Ideologie,* Kröner, II, p. 5 and Weinstock, *Humanismus,* p. 292). For Marx the monstrous power of evil which is at work in the economic disorder of capitalism to proletariatize or dehumanize man does not create itself. It comes from man and he is therefore guilty of it. Man's own act becomes for him an alien power which subjugates him instead of being controlled by him.

Is it accidental that this concept of evil is not further developed as an anthropological statement, and that (to the best of my knowledge) it never occurs elsewhere except under the sign of alienation? As I see it, the concept of radical evil is especially played down in Marxist eschatology. This offers us only a visionary picture of a man who no longer has a history. He is a remarkably unreal and docetic phantom with no features at all. At this point, where we eagerly await a picture of unalienated and authentic man, Marx simply stops portraying man at all.

What has become of the evil whose traces Marx is so aware of in historical man? Let us grant for the moment that Marx is right when he says that the social forms of dehumanizing, that is, exploitation and the class structure, are the product of evil in man. How, then, can he hope that man will change when he removes this product of his sin? Will the suppression of the act which has its origin in him alter his status? Is it not more natural to assume that the potential energy of evil will take new and different kinetic forms in the classless society, for example, individual conflicts, envy, hatred, and the desire for prestige? The aggressive impulse certainly does not change.

The picture of this eschatological authentic man is all the harder to grasp because it loses all individual features and becomes the mere substratum of a collective consciousness. As Marx himself puts it, human emancipation can be achieved only when the true individual man takes back the abstract citizen into himself, only when as an individual man he becomes a member of the species in his empirical life and individual work, only when he recognizes and organizes his own forces as social forces and therefore does not separate social force from himself in the form of political force (*Zur Judenfrage,* Kröner, p. 199).

Man achieves fulfilment, therefore, by ceasing to be an individual and becoming social man. Only thus does society bring about a unity of man's being with nature. Only thus is there affected a naturalism of man and a humanism of nature. In other words, man is brought back here to his unity with nature and the world. He wills here what nature wills and society wills. All contradictions cease, for the emancipation of the individual and the particular is ended. In the sense of Gogarten one might perhaps say that man becomes here a mythical being instead of a historical being. This leads to the cultivation of social organs, of a kind of collective instinct, through which the social will expresses itself and no longer allows man even in his spontaneity to be social and collective merely as the object of a Thou shalt (Kröner, p. 241). The socialization of the means of production will also give birth to this social man.

### g. The Great Miscalculation

Is not this man in fact an unreal ghost, a being with collective instincts and a collective consciousness? Is there any such man? Has not man as such ceased to be, becoming simply a synonym for humanity, the sum of all the positive and self-completing qualities of man?

This is where the great miscalculation is made. The nature of man, as we saw earlier, cannot be empirically transcended and achieved as a sum of qualities. But this is what Marx attempts when on the basis of the empirical course of history he presents man as economic man. Along these lines there finally arises a docetic human phantom, for the distinctive element in man cannot be grasped in terms of the particular economic expression of life. The fact that this is empirically impossible may be seen from the obvious inability to explain many human phenomena merely in terms of economic interest. Can Luther, Francis of Assisi, or even Hitler be understood in these terms alone?

Its own approach prevents Marxism from seeing the humanity of man. For, paradoxically, the humanity of man cannot be perceived so long as we focus on its immanent or functional value. At the secular level, to believe in the value of man is simply to regard him as useful, as a worker, for example, or an instrument of reproduction. It is to understand him as the means to an end.

Here we come up against a final mystery of all anthropology. In every interpretation of man there necessarily shines through the reality of man another reality, an alien element, which decisively characterizes man. This is because man can never be described except as a being in relation, a being which reaches after something and stands related to something. (By no means is this true only in Christianity.)

This alien factor (*alienum*) which determines man might be the material thing which he serves, for instance, the economic structure in Marxism or biological forces in Nazism. In this case we have some form of immanent essence. Or the alien element might be the unconditional which transcends all things, namely, God. In this case man has the alien dignity which is to be described as the essential characteristic of the divine likeness. Kierke-gaard expresses the difference between the two relation-ships when he speaks in *Sickness Unto Death* of the infinite reality which the human self acquires when it is aware of being before God, of having God as a standard, of being constituted by the divine *alienum* which is over it. The cowherd is a poor self if he is a self only in rela-tion to cows and in the same way a master is a poor self if he is a self only in relation to slaves. In fact, these are not really selves at all, since there is no standard. The child that has previously had only children as a standard becomes a self when as a man he finds a standard in the state. But what an infinite accent falls on the self when it acquires God as the standard.

### h. Authentic Humanity

The worth of the self is decided by whether the alien factor to which it is related is above or below it. If it is determined by what is below it, its own rank accords with this. The man who is controlled by things is himself drawn into the world of things. Only he who has the alien dignity which being in relation to God confers can escape the enslaving grip that values him as a thing and drops him when he no longer has utility as such. Here alone do we find the protection, the impregnability, and the sacred privileges which man has when he is recognized as the bearer of an alien worth. Even when he ceases to be useful, he is still the one whom God created. He is still, in the Old Testament term, the apple of God's eye. God himself offers protection, so that to touch him is to touch God.

Similarly in the New Testament the dignity of man is not found in outstanding people, in the great examples of the race, in the genius or moral hero, but in the lowly, in those who need mercy, in the *ptochoi*, in the extremes of the opposite and darker side.

The hidden Christ encounters us in the hungry, homeless, naked, empty, and imprisoned. He makes himself the brother of all these. To receive or visit or feed or clothe them is to do it to him. Along the same lines Paul can speak of the inviolable dignity even of those who want to restrict Christian freedom and lay burdens upon us. Christ died for them and therefore we are not to get angry with them (Rom. 14:15; 1 Cor. 8:11). The alien dignity is what makes them sacrosanct.

Here, then, man is not related to self or things or his utility but to the glory of God which wills to manifest and magnify itself in him. He is sheltered in the alien righteousness of Jesus Christ. God wills to see him in his Son. As, therefore, he has infinite worth in the eyes of God, so he is given true humanity in the eyes of men. The humanity of the Son of God who calls us brethren is hidden and shamed herein, but it is shamed and honored precisely in its hidden dignity.

It is not true, then, that man becomes small because he is a servant, that the excess of God's glory presses him down. God is not like the oriental despot who shows his greatness by degrading the slaves around him. The idea that the greatness and absoluteness of God means the littleness and devaluation of the men related to him is a false one. The very opposite is the case. The greater the object to which man is related (so long as this object is God himself and not a superior created entity which relativizes man), the more unequivocal his humanity is, and the more inviolable as such. We see this from the marginal cases of humanity which will be understood either as the apple of God's eye or as the playthings of human opportunism.

### i. The Decisive Insight

For us, then, this is the decisive insight. The image of man is always vitally stamped by the *alienum* actualized in it. This is the key to the remarkable and at first surprising fact that Marxism, in spite of its concern for man, eventually makes of him a thing. It sets him in a false relation and it is then unable to get at him through the autonomy of this relation or even to find him. It never sees man at all.

Man can be shaped by what is below him. In this case his humanity is consumed by the material *alienum* and at the last we find only the glazed face of inhuman nature or the equally inhuman because uncovered mechanism of dialectical puppets. On the other hand man can be shaped by what is above him, by the *alienum* of the divine image. In this case the goal is the impress of God's glory which chooses us as its instrument. As the glory of God addressed to us, however, this is, in the traditional vocabulary of Christianity, *gratia* or grace.

By what factor do we see the image of man stamped? In what factor do we see it sustained or would we have it lost? This is the decisive question for the west. To shed a clear light on this question, and to show on what a knife's edge the decision has been for several decades now, has been our aim in this investigation.

## B. MAN AND SOCIETY

### 1. The Worldless I

If I am right, recent thinking on man's understanding of himself and the world is characterized by two difficulties which correspond to one another and which are solved antithetically in the process of history. These difficulties consist in I-lessness and world-lessness.

The first to see and reflect on this problem seems to have been Descartes. For the high scholasticism of the Middle Ages nature and grace, the terrestrial and the supraterrestrial, were brought together in a comprehensive, static, and unquestionable system. Descartes, however, shattered this system with his methodical doubt. This doubt destroyed the certainty of the rational nexus and left as the only redoubt of direct evidence the certainty of the I: I think, therefore I am. At this first stage the relation to the outer world and also the relation between man and God were lost and nothing remained but the solipsistic isolation of the ego. Later Descartes was able to overcome this worldlessness by an ontological proof of God. Only when there is available in God the comprehensive factor which encompasses both subject and object, both thought and extension, can the I see itself freed from the arctic zone of worldless I-isolation and endowed anew with the world and being in the world.

This beginning with the I may be seen in modified form in Kant. This time it is the transcendental I of epistemology. The basic question for Kant is the structure of man's ability to know. This forces him to discuss the I as the subject of experience. In consequence there again arises a kind of worldless I-isolation. We see this especially in the *Critique of Practical Reason* in the discussion of eudaemonism and the problem of happiness. For reasons that need not be investigated here duty and happiness are at odds. They thus exclude one another as possible motives of disposition and action. Yet happiness is essential to man's self-fulfilment. It arises when things go as a rational being desires. It rests on the agreement of nature with its total end. In modern jargon, one might say that it consists in the I being identical with itself in the world, in its being allowed by the world to come to itself instead of being denied this possibility and condemned to alienation. Worldlessness as we find it in Kant consists in the fact that elimination of the motive of happiness also destroys the relation to the world which alone makes possible man's happy identity with himself.

At this point Kant's thinking proceeds along much the same lines as that of Descartes. For there now appears the *deus ex machina* who restores the lost relation and in the form of the supreme good brings about the combination of duty and happiness or person and world. This restoration of the lost relation, however, is even more questionable than in Descartes. For what the world is supposed to contribute, namely, making happiness possible, it cannot accomplish in Kant, since this would again involve the illegitimate mixing of motives which have to remain separate. Duty and happiness have to stay apart like fire and water. For this reason their combination can come only in an afterlife. In spite of complicated manipulations with the postulate of God, Kant does not succeed, therefore, in restoring the lost relation between the I and the world. The final solution lies in a prolongation of existence without the world, a welcome starting-point for later theories of social revolution.

The theological importance of these I-centered ideas seems to me to be as follows.

In both Descartes and Kant the I is the true reality, whether this be the ontological I of the former or the epistemological I of the latter. God is deduced from this primary reality of the I. It is not he who defines the I in the sense of Baader's counter-formulation: I am thought, therefore I am. God is defined by the I and in his knowability he is subject to the conditions offered by the noetic structure of the human subject. God is not grasped in the force of an experience: "Depart from me, for I am a sinful man, O Lord." He is located on a continuation of immanent lines of certainty and is used as a later aid in smoothing out the antagonisms of existence. It is no wonder that in the light of this view of God Heine describes Kant as the father of the death of God theology.

These philosophical constructs, which seek to free man from I-isolation and to restore his lost world by means of theological manipulations, find a certain continuation in modern post-Kierkegaardian existentialism. Here, too, the solipsistic I is the center. The world is simply that which alienates the I from itself and drags it down to the world. Thus in Heidegger the I that is destined for self-being becomes anonymous man. In Sartre the I is "fixed" by others, neighbors and the public, and pushed into inauthenticity. The I can achieve identity with itself only by maintaining itself against the world. Nature with its sunshine and moonlight, and history with its autonomous structure, are simply the dark background against which the light of existence shines.

It need not surprise us that these views, which have for a long time dominated modern thought and which circle around the isolated individual, unleash explosive forces when suddenly gigantic world problems overtake us, for example, when the dangerous structural relations between rich and poor, between monopolists and exploited, herald a telluric catastrophe. These problems cannot be tackled with a philosophical and theological tradition which thinks in terms of I-isolation and which is thus individualistic. Understandably a passionate protest is launched against a tradition which leaves us in the lurch when elementary questions of life direction arise, which tempts us, indeed, to ignore these questions. The theology which is caught in these patterns of thought, as Bultmann's existentialism is, comes under the same condemnation. A monstrous need arises to solve the problems of social structure and to achieve control of the world. Solutions are being sought where they can be had, or where it is thought they can be had, if not in the established sciences, then on the black market.

## 2. The I-less World

Over against the extreme of I-isolation there is the opposite extreme of an I-less secularism, if a simplification may be permitted. The Hegel-Marx tradition represents this. The absolute spirit is closer to immediacy in objective structures and institutions than in the individual, which displays the spirit only in its being for itself, in its alienation, at any rate so long as it actualizes itself only in its particularity (*Die Vernunft in der Geschichte*, Meiner, p. 70) and does not seek to be an exponent of the universal. To this extent the individual I which as an atom opposes itself to all fulfilment stands over against the total fullness of the idea (p. 69). From the very outset, then, the individual is alien to the spirit and frees itself from the universal of the idea. It finds its way back to the idea (cf. Hegel's doctrine of the individual in world history) as it makes itself a function of the world spirit and thus abandons its role as an individual.

In this tradition, then, it is the world with its structure that is absolutized. Representing the universal, the world takes precedence of the much reduced individual personality. This remains true even when Marx turns Hegel's doctrine of the spirit on its head.

It is understandable that after the domination of the individual from Kant to existentialism this different tradition should exercise considerable fascination and that Marx should have such a following. For socially and economically the modern world shows such glaring disproportion that there has to be change. The structural question is thus the burning one and the line from Descartes by way of Kant to existentialism seems to be able neither to sense this nor to offer any remedies.

The structural question is so thematized in the new school that wrong relations are found in the universal sphere which transcends the individual. Thus they have to be set right on this level, namely, by organizational change, and, if possible, change of the structures themselves. If the fault is in the capitalist system, as Marx thought, then mere patching up or individual protest is little help. The remedy, too, must have a systematic character, that is, it must change the system.

Put in terms of Christian agape this is sometimes called a political diaconate. Ministering to neighbors can no longer consist merely in direct I-Thou encounters, as in the case of the Good Samaritan. An effective suprapersonal instrumentality must be used to alter relations on a grander scale. As regards means and procedures, it is usual to speak of revolution as distinct from mere reform. Reform suggests immanent alterations in the system or tactical modifications in detail. In Marxist circles a mere concern for reform comes, therefore, under the verdict of revisionism.

Revolution, in contrast, is a strategic concept. It seeks the overthrow of a defective social, political, and economic system. Revolution can be achieved without force. This may be seen from the industrial revolution, which by technological evolution gave birth to new strata and classes. But it may also demand force when, in Marxist terms, the quantitative perversion of relations is so great that a nodal point is reached at which quantity is transformed into a new social quality.

It is undoubtedly the achievement of Karl Marx that he was the first to radically derive from a philanthropic and secularized Christian motive the task of revolutionary social change. In offering Marx this token of respect I am not suggesting that we can consider today the methods which Marx proposed for bringing about this change. I myself am inclined to agree with Max Kohnstamm, who at the Synod of the Evangelical Church in 1968 stated that he had much more confidence in the biochemical development of new wheat-strains than he had in Karl Marx as a solution to world hunger. But we need not go into that here. A thinker's questions are often more influential historically than his answers are. Criticism of the system, and the idea of new systems, we certainly owe to Karl Marx.

### 3. World Change as a Task of Christian Love

When we turn to the history of Christianity we are forced to say that its understanding of love prior to Marx (and for a long time after him) has remained essentially in the sphere of individual relations. This has been true even when the practice of love has taken organizational form as in the great societies for relief and reform.

Nevertheless, beginnings have been made which look beyond this sphere or at least set up a system of theological coordinates in which the question raised by Marx can be included. I have in view especially Luther's doctrine of the two kingdoms. Here the kingdom on the left hand, the temporal kingdom, is understood as a dimension of reality which, like all reality, stands under God, but which is also governed by supra-personal and in a sense autonomous structures. The divinely willed particularity of its composition has to be respected when one acts in this sphere. Teachers, judges, statesmen, and so forth all stand under the laws of their own disciplines and they use reason to learn these laws and to act within them (cf. *Theological Ethics*, I, p. 378, n. 1). It should not be too difficult to show that this line of thought can find a place for a view of Christian love which refers it to more than the sphere of individual relations and gives it the task of influencing systematically the laws of the kingdom on the left hand.

The real theological problem does not arise, then, at this point. Thus far the Christian tradition of thought is indeed in a good position to receive impulses from the secular sphere, for example, as regards the structural dimension of agape, and to integrate them into its theological legacy.

The point where there can be no theological integration is to be found where the justifiable structural equivalent of agape combines with a dogma of secular anthropology and is ideologized in consequence. In what does this dogma consist?

## 4. The Primacy of Structures over Man

This dogma comes to expression in a thesis which no longer offers a purely pragmatic basis for structural change, for example, its strategic effectiveness, but instead offers a metaphysical basis. On this view man is no longer seen standing over against historical structures with his own personal being as something more than a function of structurally guided processes. Instead he is a product of the structures and an exponent of their processes and laws. Without going into detail I suspect that this thesis is a development of Hegel's aversion to the individual as that which is alien to the universal of the idea. Elsewhere (*Theological Ethics*, II, 1, § 78; [no ET], n. 1) I have tried to show how this aversion lives on in Marxist anthropology and leads here, too, to depersonalizing elements.

The metaphysical axiom to which I am referring may be found in the reason advanced for the structural change demanded. This might be formulated as follows: Since man is the product of historical, for example, social and economic structures, the structures must be changed in order to change man.

This axiom may rightly be opposed as metaphysical. For in it a rigid causal sequence is postulated in which the structures have the rank of first cause and man seems to be no more than effect. Obviously this is more and other than what can be integrated into Christianity. What we had in view was diaconal action, in the name of agape, on the supra-personal conditions of human life with the aim of helping man. Here, however, on the basis of a metaphysical axiom we have action on the supra-personal causes of human life with the aim of changing man. This is the difference.

That I am not overstating the matter is shown by a critical (and self-critical) Marxist like Robert Havemann (cf. *Dialektik ohne Dogma?* 1964). For him, man is obviously no more than the product of social circumstances. This comes out very clearly when he describes the very mark of humanity, man's relation to good and evil, as a result of social situations. Good and evil are just social concepts (p. 144). Hence communist society will know no thieves or robbers. Relations between individuals are immoral only because men are dependent on one another, that is, because they are under systems which will be dismantled in communist society (p. 120). When there is no private property there will be no crime (p. 156).

Crime, guilt, and aggression are not viewed here as an innate potentiality triggered by perverted social systems. In accordance with the metaphysical axiom formulated above, they are the product of these systems. Logically, then, when the causal relations are changed, men are good and the purity of paradise comes down. Herbert Marcuse is far more realistic when he admits that in any society there will always be some personal conflicts and rivalries. For example, two men might fall in love with the same girl. We cannot imagine a society in which this does not happen. Perhaps this admission is connected with certain personal privileges which may be found in the modified Marxism of Marcuse.

In some forms of modern revolutionary theology one may undoubtedly recognize the thesis that man is the product of his relationships and consequently that historical structures do not merely help to condition his personal life but are its cause. Thus a young Hamburg pastor is reported to have made the ill-considered statement that previously theology has tried to change man in order to change the world, but now we shall change the world in order to change man. The christological implication of this is that Christ is no longer my Lord and Savior who from a grain of mustard seed (Matt. 13:31ff.; Mark 4:26ff.) causes a great tree to grow whose branches spread across the world; he is the Revolutionary who

shakes the structures of the world in order that he might
make us righteous by setting the world to rights. This
would be at odds with all that the chorus of New Testament witnesses tells us about him and would be in absurd
contradiction with all that has always been believed and
confessed in the church of Jesus Christ. But it would be
consistent with the metaphysical axiom to which we have
referred. The thing we need to be clear about is whose
consensus we are accepting and with whom we are part-
ing company.

For the rest, there may be seen in this ideologized
Christianity an ancient heresy, for it is less novel than
non-historical thinking imagines. This heresy has been
present throughout the history of the church in different
forms. I am referring to the idea of righteousness by
works. On this view man can change himself by his own
acts. He does not do what he is but is what he does. In
Luther's time the righteousness of works took an individualistic turn. It was understood as the action of an
individual. Today it is seen in collectivistic terms. Man
comes to himself when he manipulates the causative
historical structures—something which, according to
Marxist dialectic, he is able to do even though he is
their product. By manipulating them, he changes himself,
or comes to self-realization.

Soteriologically expressed, man redeems the structures from their alienation and in so doing redeems himself from his alienation too. There thus takes place what
Paul calls the relapse of the foolish Galatians from the
righteousness of faith to the righteousness of works (Gal.
3:1ff.). Redemption by Christ gives way to enslavement
by the law (4:8ff.) or the false circumcision (Phil. 3:2).
From this it is just a step to the thesis we are constantly
hearing today, namely, that now it is the structures that
must be converted and the conversion of men will follow.
I hope that I am not indulging in unkind caricature if I
take this to mean that the conversion of men is a by-
product of structural change.

## 5. The Result: A Utopian Thrust

I have tried to throw light on the theological and intellectual background against which the above thesis must be seen. I believe that this background is a terrifying one, especially when we bear in mind what has always been the Christian understanding of faith and concept of man.

These sociological doctrines of redemption necessarily lead to the construction of utopias. The reason for this is easy to see.

So long as man is seen before God, he has to be regarded as one who has fallen from God, who is alienated, and who has been expelled from paradise. History can never lead him out of this status; it can only confirm it by fresh demonstrations of his egoism, aggressiveness, and self-will. The most that he can do, and is told to do by the Lord of history, is to channel his urges and make them fruitful. Egoism, for example, can be put to productive use and can achieve an energizing quality (cf. Adam Smith's view of self-interest and Reinhold Niebuhr's *Reflections on the End of an Era*, 1934, p. 5). Recognition of the fallenness of man is one of the most vital reasons why the New Testament does not present the kingdom of God as the goal of utopian evolution in history but as something that comes from outside.

These presuppositions are abandoned, however, the moment man is regarded as a function of social conditions. Then his alienation is in principle conquerable. He can become perfect to the extent that the structures reach perfection, overthrowing domination and making possible a world of justice, of adult co-operation, and of freedom from hunger and anxiety. We know how common such utopian dreams are today.

Is it malicious to call them dreams? Do not utopias have a very realistic side inasmuch as they are very effective politically and unleash the forces of progress? Even if they are dreams, do they not have creative power in history?

They undoubtedly do, and for two reasons.

First, they do not let man remain tied to the *status quo* but set the future before him as one of open possibilities. The ontology of what Ernst Bloch calls the "Not yet" produces hope and hope gives wings. To be man is to be on the way to something different. Man as he now is can be bettered. This must be so if he is shaped by the structures and they can be bettered. Even under necessity there can be powerful impulses for pressing on in the desert.

Secondly, utopias have mobilizing power because they measure the present by the standard of imagined perfection and they condemn it in the name of this standard. They thus give rise to criticism and protest. They do this even when as goals they have no sharp contours but are simply the object of obscure pressure with no clear end in view. Even in this case they trigger the idea of a dialectic of the negative which will later of itself lead on from protest to more clear-cut goals.

Those who see the future in this utopian way, and who are thus critical of the present, can easily play an avant-garde role and downplay all others as reactionaries. Even if they are negative and destructive, few connect this with a carping spirit. The shapers of public opinion seem to think that they must be highly visionary and open to the future if they can leave the present and judge it at such a distance. If this were really so, they would be proved right by the future when it comes and they would thus achieve lasting stability. But this is not so. Nothing is more transitory than their programs. Some day a historian ought to write a history of avant-gardists and their criticisms, but I fear that he would need a slow-motion camera to do so. For the fads rise so quickly and then disappear again that the normal organs of sense, even those of a historian, cannot register them. And how comical the idols of the past are when we look back on them.

## 6. Criticism of Utopias

Let us take seriously the final dream of a world that has
been made structurally perfect, of the paradisal organization in which force and injustice are extirpated and the
domination of one person by another has ended. This end
seems to be foreshadowed already in certain welfare
states. But what kind of an end is it? In spite of all
attempts at acclimatization, will not man freeze perhaps
in this world of well-oiled machinery? Can he be more
than a contented lemur, well supplied and fully integrated
into a smooth social apparatus, when there is neither risk
nor conflict between the cradle and the grave? Can the
law behind such ideas—the law of the universal which
reduces the personal individual to nothing—do anything
but bring the course of history to a perfection in which
personality is completely suppressed, and with it that
which Marcuse would like to rescue from the repressive
tolerance of society and see regenerated? Will not this
mean  complete integration and conformism? What utopian dreams are these?

I fear that the host, that is, man, is left out of
account here. But man cannot be left out of account on
the biblical view. To repeat what we said a little earlier,
is he not still an aggressive being? Can his aggressiveness
and injustice and envy and drive for power and prestige
be explained solely by frustration at unjust structures?
Are they not part of himself, his nature? Even in Marx
himself do we not find an occasional sense of this—an
awareness that man must be investigated as well as the
structures? Does he not perceive that the monstrous force
of evil which does its alienating and dehumanizing work
in the disorder of capitalism has not arisen on its own
but finally originates on man's initiative and is man's
fault? As Marx says in the *Deutsche Ideologie,* it is man's
own act which becomes an alien power that confronts him
and subjects him instead of being ruled by him. The doctrine of structural and utopian redemption no longer sees

this fundamental ambivalence of man. It does not want to see it. Is the real issue, then, that of a conversion of structures? This is surely a rhetorical question.

To the anthropological criticism I should like to add a more narrowly theological consideration. If this whole idea is a dubious one, especially when theologians adopt it, is this not because God is eliminated here as the one who embraces both person and structure, who calls me by name and thereby makes me a person, but who also upholds the nexus of the world and makes it a responsible economy for him whom he has called by name? But if the all-embracing God is left out of account, does not everything fall apart, so that all that remains is either the Cartesian I or the impersonal nexus?

To me this is the decisive question. I will not develop it apologetically here. I will simply say that if we integrate faith in God into our ideas, order will be restored. What I said at the outset about the line from Descartes to Kant is enough to warn us not simply to drag in the thought of God at the end as a later means of mastering the contradictions of being in the world.

Instead, the only legitimate way as I see it is to study the biblical relation between God, ego, and world, and then to ask whether this relation might not serve as the summons to a new orientation.

## 7. The Primacy of Person over Structure

Of the many things that call for discussion here, for reasons of space I will simply offer a few starting-points for further reflection.

It is perfectly clear that biblical thought always begins with the person and not the circumstances of structures. The attitude of Jesus is typical in this regard. He does not turn primarily to representative people or to what nowadays is called the establishment. He is not trying to find personal keys for strategically more effective changes. He stays with the poor, the blind, the lame, and the possessed, with those who are completely without social influence. This is important in relation to our own problem because if structure rules anthropology, man is significant only in virtue of his role in the structure, whether he plays the role as an individual or as the member of a class (the working class or the exploiting class). The infinite value of the human soul before God (Harnack) is replaced by the pragmatic standpoint of utility or non-utility. For Jesus, however, every man stands directly before God, is of value to him, and is called by name.

Here, then, is a different approach to anthropology, and we can hardly accept the banal explanation that there was no sociology in those days. This initial emphasis on the immediacy of man to God is so deeply embedded in the Christian faith that its surrender means surrender of the faith too. It is of such material importance that the man who is called by his name, even though blind, lame, or of no social value, will retain his rank in any structure. He will still do so even when the structure-changing side of Christian agape is recognized and accepted as a task. I fail to see why this biblical view of man should not be the salt in this soup too!

I once tried to show in a sermon on the Good Samaritan that in this parable love of neighbor undoubtedly begins at the level of personal encounter. Finding the man who had fallen among thieves, the Samaritan sets out to help him spontaneously, unsystematically, and not as part of a program. Divine sonship and human brotherhood are the direct motives behind this improvisation of help. Both are represented in the wounded neighbor. But if the Samaritan was making this trip as a mayor or statesman, what was there to stop him from considering whether such attacks might not be prevented in the future, for example, by combing the hills for bandits and trying to find out why these social misfits had become robbers so as to get at the causes of crime? In this case we should have a model of the transition from individual and spontaneous agape to social, systematic, and structurally effective agape. But again why should not the original motive—that we have here a neighbor who is loved and valued by God—carry through into the second stage too, the stage when the seed of direct brotherly love has become a tree whose branches cover the earth, in this case the structures?

A second illustration might help.

The Epistle to Philemon tells how the slave Onesimus ran away from his master Philemon and by a remarkable coincidence came into the service of Paul. Later, when the slave had become a Christian under his influence, the apostle sent him back to his former owner. He thus returned him to slavery. Does this mean that for Paul faith is simply an inward matter which has nothing to do with the social structures within which there are masters and slaves, men and non-men? Are these structures to be left intact? Not at all!

Paul tells Philemon that now he and his slave Onesimus are brothers in Christ. This means that in their mutual relation two orders now overlap, the social order of the master-slave relation and the kingdom-of-God order of the brother-brother relation. In the long run this overlapping will cause friction. For the social order of the time can justify slavery only in terms of a specific anthropology, namely, that the slave, as Aristotle taught, is not really a man, having no soul or personality. Hence the slave, in contrast to Kantian ethics, is to be regarded as the means to an end and cannot be regarded as an end in himself. In contrast, the Christian view is that every man, even the slave, is an end in himself, being the child whom God has bought with a price, and consequently the brother.

By conferring predicates such as these on Onesimus, and commending him to his former master as a brother, Paul attacks indirectly the structural form of slavery and changes it. The extreme paradox, which Paul undoubtedly plans, is that Onesimus returns to slavery for a motive which radically opposes this structural form and necessarily erodes it from within. For this motive is that of freedom. As a free child of God, Onesimus binds himself to another free child of God within a provisional order. An explosive is thus smuggled into the structural form of slavery which will change the order and finally blow up the structure.

The core of this anthropology on its negative side is that the social structure does not define the person. If it did, the person would be eliminated, being reduced to a molecule in a collective. The positive aspect is that the understanding of the person, and the motive of agape derived therefrom, remains the guiding insight even when service to men involves a revolution in social structures. Here, too, the central content of the faith remains in force. When it is set aside, not only does the faith go, but humanity too. It is replaced by the inhuman mechanism of social apparatus and the *phobos* of utopian abstraction.

The statements of the Old Testament prophets are to the same effect. They do not proclaim a program of structural change but preach judgment and promise. Change begins as the heart is changed first, the stony heart giving way to a heart of flesh (Jer. 24:7; 31:33; Ezek. 11:19; 36:26). This changed heart is the seed of world change.

## 8. The Political Equivalent of the Christian Message

In our day many people have seen again that there is a political equivalent of the Christian message (cf. *Theological Ethics*, Vol. II). This is a legitimate rediscovery which should have come much sooner. It should be remembered, however, in whose name we are thinking here and what sign must be put before the bracket of these reflections. It would not be the first time in church history if a beginning were made in the name of a Christian motive and the next moment there were submission to an alien authority. The "German Christians" of the Hitler period are a recent example. If we fall under the sway of the false gods of an ideology, the body of Christ can no longer serve the world's salvation but is itself disrupted.

The defect of the modern theology of revolution is not that it transcends the individual aspect and recognizes the ethical significance of structures. Its failure is that it starts with structures in its attempt to change the world. It speaks of the conversion of structures and in so doing misses the point that in the strategy of God the key is the conversion of the human heart and the discovery of the neighbor.

Even if I am a planner and doer on a big scale, even if I discover just structures and achieve them, if I do not have love, I am a noisy gong or a clanging cymbal (1 Cor. 13:1). If you do not accept this simple statement of a theologian, perhaps you will listen to the prophet of shock and "happening," Joseph Beuys, who has said that true revolutions do not begin with the changing of external structures but with the changing of the individual (cf. *Christ und Welt*, No. 1, 1969, p. 13). Karl Jaspers, too, has said that the church's chances lie in the Bible if it can bring this to expression with an awareness of world change. But what does this eternal Word speak of? Where does its work begin when it changes historical situations and structures? It begins with the regeneration of man (*Die Atombombe und die Zukunft des Menschen*, 1958, pp. 356, 360).

When I give primacy to person over structure, I do not mean that first men must be converted, or must come to a new awareness of the situation, and that only then can the intellectual situation work itself out socially, structurally, and institutionally.

It is true that social and political structures usually give evidence of historical stability only when there is an intellectual compatibility with them on the part of those concerned. When this is not so, they are like an oppressive law imposed from outside and will be discarded when opportunity offers. There is a rejection process in the area of institutions too.

Nevertheless, it is also a fact of experience that new structures can change the awareness of men and therefore men themselves. While it can be very dangerous to introduce a democratic system of government before people are ready for it, in some cases the system can itself produce the necessary maturity. Similarly social legislation can foster a respect for humanity and thus help to engender a new state of mind. It is thus correct that structures can change men and open them up to a recognition of their neighbors as fellow-men.

All the same, one cannot infer from this that the causal relation of "first the person and then the structure" may be reversed. Instead we must ask: *Who* is pressing for structural change, *who* wants this first, perhaps by immediate revolution, and therefore *who* is not ready to begin by creating intellectual readiness for the new structures? Of the initiators at least we must say that they can will the new structures only because their own consciousness has reached a point where their structural postulates are possible.

If, then, structural changes can change men, the revolutionary or reforming pioneers at least must have been changed or, in some sense, "converted" before they could work out their program of structural change. If not, the role of Karl Marx is impossible to understand.

In the heads of the elite, then, there must have formed a conception of the relation between person and structure. In other words, they must have developed a specific understanding of man which has normative significance for this relation. This understanding will either respect man as unconditioned and see him as an end in himself or it will treat him as the mere bearer of a function and thus evaluate him pragmatically. On this alternative will depend whether man is made for the sabbath (i.e., institutions) or the sabbath for man (Mark 2:27).

The answer to structural questions will thus depend on the given understanding of the human person. Even on the utopian view the form of the structures will be determined by it. At issue will be either functional structures which serve, or structures which are an end in themselves and in which man functions merely as a powerless and involuntary cog. In the specific case of the Marxist utopia one wonders which is nearer the mark, the leap into freedom of Marx or the vision of Orwell.

Christian preaching and Christian theology must put this question to their partners in dialogue. They must also put it to themselves. The basic issue is who or what man is, or, more precisely, where is the ground of his being, in the Word or in structures. Here again we come up against the hidden question of God.

## C. MAN AND PHOTOGRAPHY

The camera can unmask us. Whether in so doing it discloses secrets or breaks taboos need not be discussed here. It is enough that we realize that we are living in an age which loves indiscretion and wants a direct objectification of intimacies. This is not just because we are more lascivious today or more highly sexed. The objectification of intimacy relates not merely to love but also to death and indeed to the whole range of private life.

No, as I see it the desire for disclosure and objectification rests on the fact that with the flood of images, with constant pictorial intrusion into the inner psyche, we are gradually falling victim to a loss of imagination. The psyche which can satisfy its need for images by imports from illustrated magazines and television loses a taste for its own products, so that finally the imagination almost ceases to function at all. Two examples will make this plain.

When we read again today articles or editorials which caught our breath because of their boldness in the days of Hitler, we are a little disillusioned and usually find a general conformity to the age. At any rate we find painful traces of a very mild "yes but . . ." attitude. We do not find confessions which give evidence of real opposition or of the spirit of Luther: Here I stand; I can do no other. Now why is the impression so different today from what it was yesterday? Well, in face of the elementary threat of that time our senses were sharp and receptive, so that we could catch the slightest hints. The indirect and concealed statement was enough. It had a Socratic effect. It triggered intellectual and emotional reactions in the reader and roused his own spiritual forces. But this could be so only so long as the forces were there and were ready. If we want to achieve a similar effect on the psyche today, we can no longer rely on that ability of the mind to react. Socratic hints are no good. We need a sledge-hammer to make any impression.

This is why we are so noisy, pictorial, and direct. Only little minds, which suffer from cerebral hypertrophy and a possible overhang of intellect, adopt the feeble explanation that this overkill, this insensitivity to taboos, is owed to a triumph of freedom. When we set it over against the prudery of the Victorian age, it is easy enough to make this idea of a triumph of freedom sound plausible. In truth, however, we have here a deficiency, a scurvy of the soul, and the only freedom is the freedom to ingest pictorial vitamins in order to stir the impotent imagination to action again.

The second illustration is this. It seems to me that in literature the extreme opposite of our age of noise is Adalbert Stifter. Now I hope that no one will take this to mean that I would like the new generation of authors to be a set of Stifters. This would be to make the absurd demand that literature should not grow out of the soil of the age. We know what this kind of demand can lead to from the example of neo-Gothic styles which help to hide our own lack of ability and whose incongruity simply adds to our embarrassment. Stifter is mentioned here merely as the representative of a kind of literature that we have lost and with the loss of which we have come to terms. In his world there seem to be only good men and harmonious measures. All is symmetrical. When we recall his final suicide, this should perhaps make clear what is hinted at when we read him, namely, that it is hard to believe that there could be on earth these architectural marvels with no cellars or underground vaults. Stifter was well aware of the subterranean existence of man. The dark is indirectly present in his world. We find in it terror and mystery. The reader who is not wholly insensitive will detect the presence of the stony guest. But a modern reader whose literary instinct is attuned to some of our best-sellers will find only a dull goodness with no contours. He will miss the pepper of evil, not because it is not there, but because his nose and tear-ducts are no longer fine enough to react to what is between the lines. He is so used to expeditions through psychoanalytical cellars in which what is hidden is dragged out and the darkness is lit up with high-wattage lamps and what is hardly even thought is cheerfully trumpeted abroad. In Stifter everything seems to be set in the fair light of day (as though this were possible without cellars too). But if we today do not see the termites in the underground sphere of human existence, if we do not actually hear the wolves howling in the cellar, we do not believe in them, and we blink as we find ourselves in the boring light of day.

May it not be, then, that the camera "discloses" things because we can no longer see them on our own? To be sure, this is not a rule with no exceptions. There are in fact many notable exceptions.

If the question of the background of the passion for pictorial disclosure is important, no less so is the question of what is in fact disclosed. As a momentary shot captures only a tiny particle of time, so it also expunges in part the inner dimension of the subject in so far as there is such a thing, as in cases of love and death. The empty emotional pose of a politician, the rapture of a conductor, the grieving face of a woman who has lost her son in an accident—these are aspects of a person's being, but not the being itself. Only one possibility of this being is put on view. Mostly the camera does not catch the real being, especially when in the thirst for sensationalism it tries to capture people in moments of stress. Can these momentary impressions enable us to guess how the politician plays with his children, the conductor sits over his stamp collection, or the mother reads to her grandchildren? Are not several other possibilities on the human scale not merely played down but eliminated altogether, so that they cannot even be a subject for the imagination? In contrast, is it not a feature of great art—literature as well as painting—that in its limited depiction it fashions a totality, causing us to smell and touch and hear even though no special material is offered for the nose or ear or sense of touch?

Of course there are well-known exceptions here in which what photography expresses does in fact present a kind of whole. This is so when the momentary shot has a specific symbolical rank, when the extract catches the whole and the moment the reality of life itself. An example is the wrinkled face of an old person whose folds are, according to the fine expression, the "stenography of destiny." Such a face does not proclaim merely a single moment. It tells a whole story. It rises above the contingent and becomes a valid figure. Futility, satiety, and sadness can also be caught when reporters interview certain people. Talented actors can convey the same impression too, although this is exceptional unless the cameramen are equally talented.

The other side of the coin is that the camera can also lie. It can do so even though it presents the unvarnished truth, just as a newspaper article can lie by taking things which are true in detail and putting them together in a distorting manner. Is it not a lie when a queen is seen only in the pathetic gesture of state ceremonial, or, at the opposite extreme, when she is caught

yawning, sneezing, or whispering? Is it not a lie when
the detail is taken for the whole, the beat for the melody?
Is this not a fixing of the moment, a forcing of the
moment to tarry even though it may not be so beautiful
that there is any request for this, or, on the other hand,
even though it be too beautiful to be true? Do we not have
here the very same thing as what Sartre called "fixing"
in a different connection? In some articles one can tell
at once from the accompanying portrait that the person
under discussion is a prominent or notorious one, whether
the treatment be favorable or critical. Every pore and
every wart is there. The details are what count. The total
man is fixed to the image that it is thought should be
presented, whether for polemical and pragmatic reasons
or out of a real concern for interpretation. Through things
that are right in themselves one can in some circumstances speak untruth by finding and fixing, or arranging
and fixing, the variation that is thought to be most
appropriate out of the multiplicity of those that are
available.

For myself—and perhaps I am in subjective error
at this point— I am always conscious of the ambivalence
of photography. If I put the photograph of an honored
friend on my desk, I soon grow tired of it in contrast to a
portrait, or the photograph of a portrait, on the wall.
Even when I am fascinated at first, boredom is sure to
follow. Why? In banal terms, because I do not want to
see and know with the exactitude of the shot. The lines,
the focus of the eyes, and the set of the mouth may be
exactly as they were at the moment the photograph was
taken. They may be very natural. But they are natural
only as coughing, sneezing, and laughing are natural on
the recording of a concert. On constant repetition, this
natural but accidental feature becomes tiresome, for it
always occurs at the same point and consequently it makes
an invalid claim to necessity and to the character of a
law. Recording companies are right, therefore, not to

permit on records what can be accepted, and even hailed as natural, on a broadcast or telecast.

There are many things, then, that I do not want to know exactly and do not want to have continually before me. What is lasting, the ontological background of the person, which among other things produces the accidental aspects of the moment, tends to vanish behind the things in the foreground on repeated inspection. The moment captured has to last too long. It thus dates. My knowledge of the real person increasingly comes into collision with what is caught on the photograph.

How is it that a drawing or painting has a different effect? May it be that it catches the essence of a person and not just a variation of this? Perhaps this is putting it too strongly. But this advantage at least may be granted to the portrait. What is fashioned by crayon or brush does not merely present the model but a bit of history which the artist lives through with the model. The painter is portraying his encounter with the sitter. He has to be up on him. He himself, as a spectator, is there. He brings the model into his own perspective. Perhaps we are not going too far afield if we adduce some analogies from microphysics in which the observer enters the process with his probe. He, too, is there. He does not just stand before the object. As Heisenberg puts it, he also stands before himself.

Here, too, of course, a particular aspect is seen. This is why there can be very different portraits of the same person and in the case of many historical figures of the past one cannot be sure how they themselves really looked unless one can break out of the given perspective of encounter. Yet this particularity differs from that of photography.

Since a bit of history is depicted, a bit of something lasting, which is of exemplary significance, is recorded. This is the essential being of the other as it disclosed itself in one encounter. To another it might be

different, but to me, the painter, this is the way it came
through, not just momentarily, but in a lasting manner.
This is the valid history I have with him. Love and hate
may have gone into this history as into every history.
Both can intensify the encounter. If love gives understanding, hate gives clarity. How else could caricaturists
catch the essence of people? We need them, for they
express their hate and scorn, not in accidental situation
comedy, but in such a way that in exaggerated fashion
they lay hold of what is typical. Since we can have a man
only in encounter or historically, no more is achieved than
a shadowy and deceiving exactitude when he is isolated
in an accidental moment. This is how there can so often
arise the false reporting which virtuosos of objective
photography achieve.

Perhaps I am being audacious, but surely not
unfair, if I try to set over against the photograph the
opposite extreme. I find this in Gothic art or Byzantine
icons. When a true likeness is sought in a photograph—
and many great artists of the lens attempt this—there is
a need to get at what is distinctive. Experts, who do not
have to be great artists, can put character into a weak
face by positioning and lighting effects. But when the
older painters tried to catch the essence they did not
bother about individual features. They engaged in styliza-
tion and avoided particularity. But their subjects stand
against a golden background which symbolizes the glory
of God (heaven). And a reflection of this glory shines
on their faces.

The essence, then, is to live in a relation of this
kind, to be related to the glory of God. This is the image
that God has of us—a very different outlook from the
modern one in which man is trying to get an image of
God. Here is what lasts in eternity.

The prodigal son of the parable of Jesus has to
go through many stages of exile and self-alienation. One
might snap some of these moments in his wanderings.
Possibly a film company will some day treat us to a

biblical movie along these lines. But in none of these moments is the prodigal wholly present. He is wholly present only in the picture which the sorrowing and yearning father has of him in his soul. Here, even in extreme alienation, the prodigal is still the one behind whom the golden background shines and upon whom this alien light shines even though all the lamps in his own life have gone out. He who has this essential image can then depict the exile, its stages, and its incidents, just as the father follows the way of the prodigal through the far country. In every aspect of his life there will always be something which transcends the accidental and momentary and which uses them merely as symbols. Look at some of Dürer's portraits and you will see what I mean.

At this point the analogy to the parable of Jesus breaks off. To try to depict what God knows about man is to be guilty of hubris or platonic dreaming. Man sees what is external, but God looks on the heart. We are unable to see more than what is external. If we try, we invent ideologies. But as we look at what is external we believe in what is not external, in what no eye has seen or ear heard and what has entered no human heart. This faith in man will always ask what image God has of us. And this image will immunize us against the profoundly ungodly fixing of the moment.

This implies no condemnation of photography and its ventures. It simply puts a question to photography, or, more precisely, to photographers and those who are called to live a bit of history with their fellows. They should encounter them and not just "shoot" them. At least this is what they should do if their aim is to portray and not just to report. If this encounter takes place and the photographer is ready for it, then he may take out his apparatus and catch the subject in various situations in a photographic version of the saying of Augustine: "Love and do what you like."

Or is this claim, as I fear, asking too much of photography? If so, we must resolutely make its limitations clear and not give in uncritically to fascination with its technical possibilities. Even though photographically we gain the whole world and catch it for ourselves, we might still suffer harm in our souls.

## D. MAN AND POWER

### 1. Power as a Supposed Evil

The problem of power has many aspects that we cannot go into here. Two of these are its perverted exercise and influence as we see them in ideological governments on the one side and on the other side in the autonomy of processes which seem to reduce to a minimum the radius of voluntary intervention. But instead of discussing these actualizations of the power problem and attempting an attractive differentiation between the power of men, institutions, and things (or processes), in what follows we shall deal with a few fundamental questions (on the ideological exercise of power cf. *Theological Ethics*, Vol. II).

A familiar fact is that Jacob Burckhardt has defined power as evil in principle. He holds this view because he is convinced that having power always carries with it an autonomous urge not merely to hold it but also to take steps to keep it. Thus the state has a permanent urge to round itself off. It makes what are thought to be necessary border adjustments, takes over smaller territories, and becomes an armed camp. This involves an expansionary trend. Again, having power leads to an ideological vindication of the right to it, as may be seen at an extreme level in ideological tyranny and totalitarianism. Finally, having power means the setting up of long-range goals and the invoking of the indirect excuse of history for any means that serve to achieve them. Lord Acton gave expression to this view that power is evil in principle when he formulated the axiom that power corrupts and absolute power corrupts absolutely.

It is doubtful, however—we must say this in criticism of Burckhardt—whether one should defame a law of the historical process or an element of historical life as evil, or whether one can ascribe demonic properties to it. For surely the judgments good and evil by their very nature can apply only to persons. Only individual men and their actions can come under moral evaluation. For there can be no moral assessment apart from a consideration of motives, and these apply only in the case of individuals. It thus follows that one cannot pass moral judgment on an anonymous historical process and its success or failure (L. Kolakowski, *op. cit,* pp. 106f.). When a something replaces the person, the danger arises that man will be released from his responsibility and be understood as the mere function of a mythical force.

In Burckhardt power does in fact become an entity which has the rank of a historical subject and which threatens to degrade man to a mere object. In face of this hypostasizing of power a demythicizing job is needed. Without doing this expressly here, we may indicate the heart of the matter by a counterthesis: Power as such is neither good nor evil. It is no more good or evil than the libido or technology is good or evil, divine or demonic. Only when man does not see his own horizon, the horizon defined by judgment and grace, the fall and redemption, does he make the mistake of finding in good and evil the properties of things, spheres of life, laws, and other areas outside himself. Only then does he begin to speak of tragic processes instead of guilty decisions.

To say this is not to deny that there are tragic processes. But these are in some way set in motion by men. They do not just happen as tyche and moira. They are not tragic from the very outset (cf. Matt. 18:8b). Man imparts their ineluctability to them. The Fall is the starting-point for autonomous processes. A dreadful inevitability arises as the first taking of the forbidden fruit leads to fratricide, fratricide to open apostasy, apostasy to the Tower of Babel, and the Tower of Babel to the overthrow of Sodom. Thére is no stopping now. Depicting the initiation of the process, the Fall is the model of something which constantly repeats itself prototypically. It offers an interpretation of history (cf. E. Auerbach, *Mimesis*, 1953), just as Goethe does in his *Sorcerer's Apprentice*, in which the apprentice unleashes forces which he cannot control and then comes under the power of the spirits which he invokes. In the same way when we open a door which has no latch on the other side, once we are through we have to go on. The past cannot be revised. It is like a switch-point which sets our course and thus gives it a certain ineluctability. The pathos of Sartre's doctrine of freedom derives essentially from its rejection of the determination which my past and its decisions impose on me and which through these thrusts me into functional dependence and thus robs me of existence. Orestes, in Promethean defiance, takes the same line when he states: I am my freedom, that is, I will not be the object of my past but I will be the subject of a new future grasped by me. I will not accept myself as a tablet which has already been written on, which has been filled up with scribbled mortgages. I will begin as an empty slate and do my own writing.

In this sense the concept of original sin tells us that the opened doors, the switched points, the initial steps are already behind us, no matter whether the determining factor is a past event and we are already in a preformed historical milieu or whether it is we ourselves who have taken the initial steps. In this process from original freedom to the inevitability of the process there may be seen the Christian view of time in which it has the form of an irreversible line running from the Fall to judgment. When the Fall is no longer in view, however, only the processes are seen and not the one who initiates and sets them going.

Here an important theological insight may be referred to in passing. The only alternative to the Fall is myth. This means the mythicizing of powers and processes. In this connection mythicizing means that things are interpreted as divine or demonic forces and are thus made into living beings. At the same time human existense is dehistoricized (in Gogarten's sense). Man becomes merely a fellow-traveler of processes, that is, a function.

Theologically myth is a movement of repression or evasion. Man sees himself here as one who is innocent in the hands of forces which sweep him away. It is in his own interest to hide his own hand and its guilty initiatory act.

We shall not stop to ask how man tries to check his dangerous power—a power which he knows to be dangerous even in mythological categories. We now realize that the more accurate form of the question is this: How does man try to check and control himself in his own jeopardizing by power? Keeping this nuance in view, we hope we can come up against the same theological problem from the other side.

There are two essential requirements for this control of power. The first is principial and the second institutional. The principial requirement is that power must be characterized by authority. The institutional requirement is that power must be shared. In the next section, then, we shall deal with the nature of authority and in the third section we shall turn to the balancing of power.

## 2. Power and Authority

Power as authority is the direct opposite of power as sheer force (cf. E. Gerstenmaier, "Wider die Ächtung der Autorität," *Reden und Aufsätze*, II, 1962, pp. 41ff.). Power as force rests on dynamic superiority. It is typified by terror, which does not try to win or convince people but simply compels them. The mark of power which is understood as force is that it makes those dependent on it into mere agents. The one who possesses force is stronger, and those governed by him, whether individuals, groups, or whole nations, are weaker.

Understanding himself in this way as an agent, man is reduced to an object—the object of operations and of the force used by him, for example, in the form of the working force expended. He can be a subject in the personal sense only if he is not compelled to function but won over to cooperation as a partner. But to win a man is to convince him. This in turn is to regard him as one who makes and carries out decisions instead of seeing him as a mere object of another's will. But the person in power is not prepared to convince others and win them over. There are two main reasons for this.

First, winning people over means work, diversion, and delay. The one who does not want to trample over others but to claim their support has to subject himself to the labor of constant self-vindication. It is more rational and economical simply to command. Even when military service is regarded, as it should be, not as a sphere of blind force but as one of authority, the rational element in refusing to explain oneself and win others over may be illustrated by military orders. In war or danger everything must be done quickly. There is no time to win subordinates over, to offer moral justification for what is proposed, or to secure agreement to dangerous operations. This would put the initiative in the hands of the enemy. Hence orders must be issued. For this reason the outbreak of violence and the degrading of subordinates to mere objects is particularly dangerous.

Secondly, the readiness to accept others as persons and let them make their own decisions involves the risk that they will say No, that they will not function, that they will not go along.

The greater effort and the greater risk need not be undertaken by one who wields superior and cynical power because in virtue of the force at his command he can make others dance like puppets on his own strings.

The one who regards power as authority, however, takes a completely different position.

Lessing's *Education of the Human Race* might serve as an example. Here God is understood in the strict sense as one who bears authority. It is true that he claims authority for himself in the early days of the race. He issues commandments and performs miracles in order to demonstrate his authority. But he does not execute blind and arbitrary decisions. He acts in the name of a reason which is not yet accessible to immature humanity but into which humanity is ripening. Hence God uses his authority to make possible an imparting of reason for which humanity is not yet ready on its own at this stage of development. By this impartation, however, he bends the development of men to a historical goal at which they will have the pure gospel of reason at their disposal and will thus become autonomous.

As Lessing sees it, the authoritarian power of God has two essential features.

First, this authority does not use power capriciously but achieves its own authorization by setting itself in the service of reason, which is above both God and man. (On the question whether God himself is subject to final norms of truth and goodness or whether he himself sets these norms cf. the famous debate between Aquinas and Scotus, or between Thomists and Scotists.)

Secondly, the authority of God is marked by the fact that it leads to autonomy and seeks to make itself superfluous. Along good Enlightenment lines it is viewed as the authority of a teacher who has the same aim as that toward which the development of the student presses. Hence a student gives poor thanks to his teacher if he always remains a student. The teacher is teaching him to stand on his own feet.

This brings us up against a relation between authority and autonomy which we might not have expected at first. For our usual view of authority is that those subject to it must give up some part of their own sovereignty and delegate it to the authority. The new relation between authority and autonomy may be formulated in two theses which we shall discuss separately. The first is that authority is always granted, or recognized, by autonomy alone. The second is that authority demands and claims autonomy alone.

(a) As regards the first thesis, authority, in distinction from blind force, is present only when the one who has it finally stands on the same level as the one over whom he has it.

This may be seen in the authority of the judge at a trial. He represents authority to the extent that he conducts the trial and acts on the commission of the legal community. But this does not place the accused in dependence on his will. It makes him his partner in the law. Both stand under the same binding law, the one as its vindicator and the other as its actual or alleged transgressor.

This partnership between judge and accused under something higher which covers both has always been the subject of basic considerations in jurisprudence which can also lead to decisions in specific cases.

An example is the handling of the question of lie-detector tests in trials. The jurist Eberhardt Schmidt (among others) argues against such tests on the ground that they undermine the position of the accused as a partner and reduce his role in the judicial process to that of an object.

The fact that the judge has to support his verdict is also to be explained along these lines. It is not so much a technical matter or a matter of showing the legal community that the verdict falls under existing laws. The main point is that the accused is addressed. The aim is to convince him that the judgment is just and thus to bring him back into the society of law which gives force to the demand for an accounting.

Whether or not the accused is convinced is of little importance compared to the fundamental position which

is adopted toward the accused, namely, that of an appeal
to consensus and the addressing of the accused as the
potential judge of his own act. In this way the law respects the autonomy of the lawbreaker and associates him
with the judge on an equality under the authorizing law.
In this the correlation of authority and autonomy is plain.

The same phenomenon may be seen in other figures and institutions representing authority.

When Luther is given some kind of authority in
the Evangelical Church it is not because of his blue eyes
and golden hair but because he speaks in the name of
Holy Scripture as the court which gives him authority.
But to the extent that this authorization is taken seriously, he is an authority only inasmuch as he stands with
all Evangelical Christians under the authority of Holy
Scripture and may be checked and controlled by it.
Luther has to be tested by Scripture just as the verdict
of a judge has to be tested, and if need be revised, by the
law.

This brings to light an essential feature of authority. It is not just in correlation with the autonomy or
maturity of those under it. It is also an impermanent
authority in virtue of this correlation. It is authority only
for the time being, that is, so long as it checks out positively against the superior court.

That Luther saw his own authority in this way,
that he wanted to be tested and refused to play the role
of a church father, has been shown by K. Holl in his essay
"Luthers Urteile über sich selbst" (*Gesammelte Aufsätze
zur Kirchengeschichte,* I, 1932, pp. 381ff., esp. 396ff.).
Once when Melanchthon said in a harmless way that they
had followed Luther's authority in a certain matter,
Luther would not accept this. Melanchthon did not mean
any wrong, but Luther would not listen to the expression.
He also renounced publicly supporters who believed only
because of him. Sound people would remain in the word
even if they heard that Luther himself had gone astray.
He was happy, then, when he heard that his own reputa-

tion was of less account, and it gave him satisfaction in the Wartburg to think that things could now be seen going ahead without him. In the same way Reformation confessions view themselves only as secondary norms which themselves have to be tested by the primary norm of Holy Scripture.

Indeed, even Scripture does not claim authority in the sense of declaring itself to be the final court of appeal. We do not believe in Christ because of Scripture but in Scripture because of Christ. This statement sums up the Reformation understanding of Scripture.

As stated thus, the correlation or partnership between authority and autonomy, which results from a third thing above both, poses a new problem. For it seems to posit equality between those who have authority and those over whom they have it. Yet the essence of authority undoubtedly consists in superordination. Prestige attaches to authority. How can these things go together?

The solution to the apparent contradiction is that we have here the overlapping of two dimensions of human reality. The one is the dimension of principle, which has *a priori* validity, and the other is the dimension of experience, which has *a posteriori* validity.

The postulate resulting from the first dimension is this. Since autonomy and personality are not destroyed, and since men or groups are not to become mere objects of force, there is an ultimate equality between those who are subject to it.

The thesis of the second dimension is different. It has been shown thus far that those who bear authority over me are right, that they have stood thus far in a relation of greater directness and knowledge to the authority that is above us both than I have. In the first instance, then, I accept the validity of what authority proclaims or commands. To that extent I acknowledge its superordination.

Authority, then, is a phenomenon which crops up in experience and temporality. This is why we use a term like "in the first instance." This means that I accept it until the opposite is proved, that is, until my adult and autonomous relation to the third thing which authorizes may make me a critic of the authority.

Hence the superordination of authority does not rest on treating its subjects as children or robbing them of their autonomy. It rests on the advance credit which adults give it because it has proved itself in their experience. For this reason we cannot speak in this connection of the authority of parents in relation to children or owners in relation to pets. For in these cases there is no experience which might lead to criticism, nor adulthood which can recognize authority. Instead we have a superordination of influence, the force of love, parental power, or the ability to train.

As experience gives an advance credit to authority, it does so to tradition too. The concepts are related. For tradition stores up the treasures of the experience of past generations. Thus the credit which our own experience grants to higher collective experience is at its disposal until the treasure of traditional experience possibly finds an adequate equivalent in our own experience or is refuted or limited by our own encounter with life—for there is in it an element which can be transcended in principle, as in the case of the dogmatic tradition of the church. In history there is always a conservative element, since history sets us in experience which has been handed down. Conservatism, however, means absolutizing of the tradition and denies our adulthood. It thus corresponds to the position which arises when authority is absolutized, when it is thus reduced to mere form, and when man sinks to the level of a mere function of force.

Only from the double standpoint that authority is equal in principle but superordinate empirically does it make sense to furnish authority with power. This is tested power related to that by which it is tested. One can entrust power to authority. One does so in order to offer it the power of free development on the basis of attestation and in terms of a credit.

For the element of experience in the rise of authority, Nehru is an excellent example. He says about Gandhi, a man of supreme authority, that once there were many who opposed him but they soon saw that he was right. They thus surrendered more and more to his judgment, having learned to rely on his principles (cf. T. Mende, *Gespräche mit Nehru*, 1956, p. 22). For the rest, Nehru is a good example of the fact that authority counts on adulthood and helps to promote it. For he himself followed a path that was independent of Gandhi.

This adulthood in relation to authority may be seen especially from an extreme example in the case of Luther. Faced with passages in the Bible which he found difficult, Luther said that one should give a respectful tip of the hat and pass on. Adulthood expresses itself here in the resolve to pass on, the ongoing authority of Scripture in the tipping of the hat, that is, the recognition that its knowledge of God is greater than one's own, so that one might have to come back later to this passage which is set aside for the moment. The object of faith is always greater than faith itself.

The advance credit in relation to Scripture can never be overdrawn. This gives it unique authority. No man can exhaust Holy Scripture. As Luther put it, one can understand Virgil's *Bucolics* and *Georgics* after five years of farming, and Cicero after twenty years in public affairs, but to know Scripture one would have to rule the churches a hundred years with the prophets (*Enders Briefe*, XVII, 60, 1ff.).

We thus maintain that the fact that authority can be recognized only by autonomy means that it is accepted on the basis of one's own insight into that which authorizes it and on the basis of the independent diagnosis of experience. It enjoys superordination, but can be criticized in principle, since it is subject to control. It can also be revised in principle, since some of its claims may later be reassessed, dispensed with, or suspended.

This distinction throws light on the two forms of authority, outer and inner. There is an official authority which in ideal cases coincides with inner or personal authority. Both forms are to be defined in accordance with our finding both in principle and empirically.

In principle the bearer of both official and personal authority stands under the same binding norms as those under him. Empirically the power of office gives an advance credit to the office-bearer which applies to him personally too, being granted to his inner authority and not just his outer authority. In general, judges, teachers, and political representatives are serious people and the social order rests on teachers being over pupils, masters over apprentices, and parents over children. The fifth commandment does not establish these relations of super- and subordination but simply confirms relations familiar already from experience. It brings the authorizing Word of God to them as the same Word comes to the water of baptism.

This gives the person of the office-bearer an advance credit. This credit applies until he proves his unworthiness to bear authority. For judges can be brought under discipline, teachers dismissed, and parents deprived of their rights when the verdict of adulthood is in. We thus see that outer and inner authority are simply two variations of the concept of authority in general and are both covered by our previous analysis.

(b) As regards the second thesis, namely, that authority claims autonomy alone, it is to be noted that the distinction between authority and tyranny is that the former finds its correlate in the free person and the latter in the slave. From what we have said about the possibility in principle of criticizing and revising authority it follows that there can be only relative dependence on it. The one who is relatively dependent owes it both to himself and also to authority that he should maintain his freedom. In this sense Socrates is a model of authority, since he teaches his students to be themselves and to cut the umbilical cord.

This maintaining of freedom by the dependent rests on the presupposition of a self-restriction of authority. We see, however, that those who have power are caught in a desire to expand and increase it and that authority is a specific form of power. We thus face a problem. How can there be a self-restriction of authority which withstands the autonomy of power? How can the ethical opportunity to be an authority be seized amid the pressures of power?

The answer certainly cannot be that the subjective virtue of modesty makes this self-restriction possible. The objective character of the pressures at work in expansion —Burckhardt is essentially right here in spite of the mythicizing obfuscation—must be restrained by another form of objectivity, namely, the embedding of authority in higher ontic relations and not just in itself, in a mere disposition of readiness for asceticism. In fact the essence of authority lies in this embeddedness, this awareness of being encompassed.

What this higher thing is we learn when we put the question more precisely: How can the desire of authority to maintain the freedom of subjects be fulfilled?

The partnership sought in this desire is possible only on one condition, namely, that authority and the partner both come under a third thing. In other words, authority can uphold the freedom of subjects only when it is authorized and validated by a norm to which subjects too stand in immediate relation.

We came up against this norm in the previous section when we discussed the question of equality. We must now think through more closely the relation which establishes authority. To do this we shall make use of a model of authority.

Paul refers repeatedly to the limitation of his apostolic authority. He sees himself forced into this by the requirement that members of the community should be adult (or autonomous) enough to be in direct relation to the third thing in question, namely, the gospel, so that they can become independent of his apostolic authority. He represents this view of authority even when he does not find the postulate of maturity fulfilled.

Thus Paul sees his apostolic authority discredited when the Corinthians who had been taught by him prove to be so suggestible that they blindly and uncritically follow any new teacher or message. This simply shows that they are not yet adult. Paul, however, is not pleased when some of the Corinthians attach themselves to him and his message. If someone comes and preaches another Jesus than he had preached, or if they receive another spirit than they have received, or if they accept another gospel than they have received, they are easily deceived (2 Cor. 11:4).

In this complaint one catches a note of annoyance that the Corinthians are not just immature but that they are compromising apostolic authority as a result. They are subject to passing influences which work only for a moment and then yield to others. Authority, however, presupposes maturity or autonomy. Without this it ceases, or does not really begin, to be authority.

For this reason Paul paradoxically displays his apostolic authority most strongly when he claims the adulthood of his hearers and exposes himself to the possibility of being questioned. The more he points to the court which authorizes him (and thus opens up the possibility of being questioned), the stronger is his claim to authority. For he is sure that he will stand before this court and that he has the gospel on his side. He thus tells the Galatians not to rely on his authority should he, or an even greater than he, namely, an angel from heaven, preach to them another gospel (Gal. 1:8). By saying that he or an angel would be accursed in this eventuality, he is demanding that the Galatians should not rely on authority figures but on that which authorizes them, namely, the gospel. His authority consists solely in the fact that he can stand up to this questioning by those who are mature.

Authority, as distinct from tyranny, is by nature a norm that is set under another norm. More precisely, we should say that it must see itself as a norm which is being shaped by another norm, since its being an authority is never in the perfect tense. It does not have an indelible character. For all the confidence we have in its experienced attestation, it has to be constantly confirmed afresh by those who are mature. Hence it never gets beyond the stage of having to be constituted anew. It thus allows those subject to it the freedom of either criticizing or affirming it in virtue of their direct relation to the ultimate norm which makes it normative.

## 3. Power and the Separation of Powers

Like the freedom which it presupposes and the trust which it demands, authority is a moral entity. Hence it cannot be forced. This opens up the possibility that there can be rule without it, for example, in the form of terror, of uncontrollable force which has gained a monopoly. In this case authority and trust are not present. Without them there is nothing to guarantee control of power. But the danger of power is well known. So is the inclination of human nature to misuse power. Institutional safeguards are thus needed to guard against this misuse.

The method employed by political theorists and constitutions to achieve this end is the familiar one known as the separation or balancing of powers. Theologically one might say that the separation of powers is an institutional expression of permanent mistrust of power, or, more accurately and less in the style of Burckhardt, of those who hold it. To call for a separation of powers is to recognize either consciously or unconsciously the reality of the Fall and the questionable nature of fallen man.

Even when state sovereignty demands a fundamental unity of supreme power, lest the state degenerate into a cover organization for conflicting forces, the way in which this power operates must be so regulated that there is achieved a balance of partial powers checking and controlling one another and yet also working in concert. For an example of the restraint that can be exercised by this separation and balance one might think of the traditional British policy of the balance of power in relation to warring European states. What we have here is an artificially contrived and institutionally effected mechanism of control, which K. Lorenz might say is a necessary human equivalent of the control by instinct which is found in the animal world. The model of a separation and balancing of powers in a state is provided by the French constitutional theorist and politician Montesquieu in his *Esprit des Lois* (1748), in which he proposes that power should be divided into three branches: the legislative branch, the executive branch, and the judicial branch.

State power as such is indivisible. But it should be portioned out to different agents. There are two reasons for this.

First, an accumulation of power at one point, whether this point be a man, an institution, or the people itself, must be avoided. Safeguards against the monopolizing of power are needed. Man's tendency to misuse power demands its restriction. Fallen man cannot handle the temptation which power brings.

Secondly, a division of power is needed to bring those who bear it—for example, president and congress, majority party and opposition, official power and unofficial powers such as the media—all under a system of mutual controls and to put the urge for power into a mechanism of restraint. The separation should not give the impression, of course, that the state is simply an umbrella for various independent and sovereign forces which all have their own commissions and which are simply to be brought together in a certain political co-ordination.

The decisive point is that state power as such is indivisible. This indivisible power is simply delegated to different organs working together in its name and on its authority. State power is not the end result of a coordination of independent forces. It is the starting-point of delegation. The state is the original delegator, not the subsequent coordinator.

## 4. Conclusion

The main results of our brief discussion are as follows:

1. The myth of what is thought to be antonomous power must be demythicized. The theological theme at issue is not power but those who hold it. Power is not insatiable or filled with a lust for expansion but the wielders of power are.

2. The questionable nature of man, who is not whole but fallen, and who must be understood in terms of the Fall as well as creation, points to the fact that power is dangerous in his hands and can be a temptation. Possession of power can have negative as well as positive results. Man is especially threatened in the technological (and nuclear) age, since technology heightens the possibilities on both sides.

3. Hence those who hold power must be restrained and controlled. We have mentioned two ways of achieving this, the inner limitation of power by its definition as authority and the outer limitation of power by the institutional means of a separation of powers. Both forms of restriction are to be seen against their anthropological background. They make sense only when it is understood that those who hold power are not to be trusted because the holding of power intensifies the questionable nature of man and carries with it destructive consequences.

There is no place here for a last and decisive chapter on a theology of power. But the theme of such a chapter may at least be indicated.

Possession of power creates distance. The most

familiar sign of this is the isolation of the rulers of this
world. By developing a jealous and suspicious guarding
of interests, power thus threatens to break communica-
tions between men and to become the opposite of love,
which is the original link in all communication. The
figure of Christ rises above this polarity of power and
love because the two are one in him. He to whom all
power is given in heaven and on earth is also he who
loves and who is unselfishly open to the very poorest and
weakest. This is, as it were, an ethical variation on the
doctrine of the incarnation.

# IV

# The Question
# of Truth

## 1. Is the Question of Truth Foreign to the World?

In his famous statement "What is truth?" Pilate questions the question of truth. As Oswald Spengler sees it (*The Decline of the West*, II, 1945), this is the only "racial" saying in the New Testament. For it opposes irreconcilably the world of facts and that of truths. It does so with more terrifying clarity and impressive symbolism than anything else in world history. For there is no bridge between time and timeless eternity, between the course of history and the existence of a divine order. In the former the Roman crucified the Galilean. In the latter Rome fell under condemnation and the cross was the pledge of redemption. This was God's will. What religion calls truth, then, is metaphysics. But one cannot adopt an appropriate attitude to this world in the name of metaphysics. The truth it has in mind, and even its question, does not conform to the world. When they are raised in the schema of the world, for example, in politics, they are felt to be a foreign body and are thus repulsed. Truth and reality are diametrically opposed. Pilate's question, then, has an ironical undertone, at least according to Spengler's understanding.

Does it follow, therefore, that the question of truth, at any rate when it relates to the dimension of ultimate reality, is from the very outset foreign to reality?

I can audaciously imagine a fascinating dialogue in which Albert Camus takes a very different view. (I deliberately choose Camus as the speaker since he can hardly be suspected of theological prejudice.)

For Camus there is certainly a type of the true which is indifferent to reality. This is the type which oddly enough aims to make statements about reality and to measure it quantitatively. For Camus, in his discussion of the absurd, it includes the scientific truth of Galileo. Galileo could in good conscience repudiate astronomical truth when it became dangerous to him, when it threatened the reality of his life. It was not worth it. On the other hand there are many people who die, says Camus, because they do not think life is worthwhile. Others again paradoxically let themselves be put to death for ideas or illusions which are for them a reason for living, for the existence of reality. What is called a reason for living is also a reason for dying. I thus conclude, says Camus, that the question of the meaning of life is the most urgent of all questions.

But the question of the meaning of life is identical with that of the truth which determines life. This truth, however, is not one among others, such as Galileo's astronomy. This truth is the ultimate truth which sustains all other truths. It has to do either with empowering for life or with the sentence of death. Hence it determines life to an eminent degree. The Roman procurator had thus no reason to put his question: "What is truth?" with an ironical undertone as though it were foreign to reality and could not be alloyed, as it were, with earthly metals. On the contrary, the truth sought in the question of meaning will decide whether we can stand reality. It is thus the basis which upholds all reality.

## 2. The Different Forms of Truth

Who is right, Spengler or Camus?

Perhaps we can think through the matter further if we leave aside for the moment the relation between truth and reality and try to distinguish the different forms of truth. It might be, as indicated by the difference between Galileo's truth and the truth of meaning, that we have variations in the concept of truth which themselves enable us to see different modes of the relation between truth and reality.

Along these lines it seems to me that there are three forms of truth which I will characterize, rather summarily, as follows: (1) There is a truth which we can know, (2) a truth which relates to us, and (3) a truth which understands us before we understand ourselves.

(1) What we know and can state in a verifiable synthetic judgment has to be objectifiable. To this belongs the character of accuracy. Something appropriate is here related to what is before us, as Heidegger points out in his essay "Die Frage nach der Technik" (*Vorträge und Aufsätze*, 1954, p. 15). To be accurate a statement does not have to disclose the nature or meaning of the thing. Only when this disclosure takes place do we have the true. Hence the accurate is not in itself the true. The latter alone brings us into a free relation to that which affects us in terms of its nature.

This would lead directly, of course, to the second of our forms of truth, that which relates to us, were it not that an intermediate question should first be discussed or at least indicated. This question is as follows: Does that which relates to us arise only through the fact that we seek the nature and meaning of what we know accurately? Or might it not be that what is accurate itself relates to us already? We take it for granted today that we have an absolute and unconditional right to gather knowledge, to extend indefinitely what we know to be accurate. As Auden says, the gossip column is one side of the coin and the cobalt bomb the other. We readily admit that eating and sex, while beneficial in moderation, are harmful in excess, but we will not agree that intellectual curiosity is an appetite too, and that knowledge is not the same thing as truth. Extension of the categorical imperative to the sphere of knowledge, so that we ought not ask what we can know but instead ought to ask what we should know at this moment, considering whether the only right knowledge which can be true for us is that to which we can do justice in our lives: this seems to all of us to be crack-brained and even immoral. For it apparently stands opposed to the autonomous chain-reaction of expanding investigation.

We are thus faced by the problem of whether even the question of the accurate does not have as such an existential reference apart from the question of nature and meaning. Does it not perhaps expose us to the possibility that we are not able to cope with what is known and its technical use? Our accurate information about atomic relations and the structure of life, and the possibility of putting this to use in physics and chemistry, may be beyond us. Space exploration possibly confirms the fact that biologically man is defective because he does not measure up to his opportunities. If so, there is no such thing as a neutral truth of knowledge which leaves our existence intact. The truth of knowledge, or even the resolve to acquire it, triggers responsibility. It poses the question of how we will relate to it, what meaning it will have for us, and what way we shall take with it.

It is thus evident that the transition from the first form of truth to the second is a fluid one and that there is no sharp line of division between the two.

(2) A few things must now be said in explanation of the second form of truth, namely, the truth that relates to us.

This has to do directly with the meaning (or nature) of things. This may be in the form of the meaning that sustains us or of meaninglessness as that which either crushes us or, being absurd, provokes our opposition and is thus creative (Camus and G. Benn).

Meaning and meaninglessness always incarnate themselves in persons. Being human or being a person finally involves my relationship to the meaning which sustains me or the meaninglessness which crushes me. Personhood is distinguished ontically by the fact that what is at issue in being is being itself (cf. Heidegger's *Being and Time*, 1962). One might even say that existence *is* a relation of this kind. This relation is its truth. Plato saw it thus when he took the question of truth to be the question of what really is in contrast to phenomena, and also when he found the essence of man in the relation he either has or does not have to what really is. On having or not having this relation depends real life on the one side or subjection to the confusion of appearance on the other.

Since this relation of existence to being or meaning, to that which embraces and transcends all that is, cannot be objectified, I cannot explain personal life but can only understand it. This distinction between scientific explanation and intellectual understanding has become a common one under the influence of Dilthey. What understanding means here in contrast to explanation is that insight into another personal life needs a certain existential pre-condition, namely, that I myself as a person represent the same structure of existence as that other personal life. Only because I have a relation to being and meaning can I understand the other in his corresponding relation. Only for this reason are his boredom and emptiness, his anxiety, his missing or achieving of being, familiar to me. Only for this reason do I understand that this other existence, like myself, is called upon to grasp his destiny, and that it runs the risk of failure. Solidarity with the other in the same type of existence makes understanding possible.

In his work on hermeneutics, Dilthey described this psychologically as a kind of sympathy not unlike the divinatory understanding of Schleiermacher. The ability to understand in this way rests on the relation of the expositor to the author which is heightened by life with the author in the form of diligent study. The concept of sympathy is simply a psychological reflection of the ontic solidarity which consists in the fact that both expositor and author are bearers of personal life. They are together in the relation which constitutes the essence of existence. Bultmann is closer to the ontological secret of understanding when he says that a living relationship of the expositor to what is stated directly or indirectly in the text is the necessary presupposition (*Glauben und Verstehen*, II, 1952, p. 215). At least in poetic, philosophical, and especially kerygmatic texts, this theme is the ultimate reality to which both author and expositor relate and which is intelligibly set forth in the ciphers of the text. The process of understanding can be intensified and refined by a certain "musicality" which expresses that which evokes the sympathy of the recipient. But this can take effect only within the ontic solidarity. It cannot replace it. If the ontic solidarity is absent, which is possible in limited form, as when, for example, I am confronted by an alien exposition of existence, musicality will provoke only an aesthetic reaction which completely misses the real point. We can see this in purely aesthetic interpretations and evaluations of Bach's oratorios by secularized admirers.

(3) Finally, we must look at the third form of truth, namely, the truth which understands us before we understand it. As Paul puts it in 1 Corinthians 13:12, we learn to know this truth as and when we are known by it. In these terms I can know the truth only when I see it incarnate in a person, in the King of truth (John 18:37f.). Apart from this I may indeed speak of a truth which discloses itself to me—the literal sense of *aletheia* —or of a truth which relates to me. But a truth which knows me and consequently sees me can be only a communication with a living other that is opened to me. This living other cannot, of course, be one to whom I stand in the general solidarity of a like constitution of being, that is, one which, like me, stands in a relation to meaning, to ultimate truth. If it were, I might say that this other had known me before I knew it, just as my mother

knew me before I knew her. But I could not say that the truth, which is at issue here, knew me before I knew it.

In fact we have to speak of the relation of Christ to the truth in a very different and indeed exclusive way. At an important point he is no longer in solidarity with me here. The exceptional character of Christ as the New Testament sees him is that he does not just represent a relation to meaning, or, as one might say, the logos. Instead, he is the Logos. The truth is incarnate in him. It is identical with him. Truth is what he is. The final reality which gives meaning is there in him, namely, the *pistis* or faithfulness of God which according to Romans 3:3 constitutes the truth of God and which is thus something which endures, on which one can rely, and which as righteousness stands opposed to man's falsehood (cf. Bultmann's article on *aletheia*, *TDNT*, I, 1964, p. 238).

Christ does not just proclaim the truth of the faithfulness of God which sustains our life and gives it permanence and meaning. This truth takes bodily form in him and is among us. He is thus characterized by "is" judgments which articulate his being and not his acts: I am the way, the truth, and the life (John 14:6); he is our peace (Eph. 2:14).

## 3. The Different Modes of Appropriation

Naturally this idea of truth in person raises wholly new problems of knowledge and appropriation, that is, wholly new epistemological questions. We do not try to explain personal life in scientific terms but see it grounded in the solidarity of common existential situations. In the same way another new and different mode of understanding arises in face of the fact that Christ is the truth, and that he does not fit, therefore, into our existential situation. I cannot understand Christ merely as I understand other men.

The new existential situation which determines him, namely, that he does not just relate to the truth but is the truth, may be seen also in what, following Dilthey, one might call the psychological reflection of this situation. There can be no meaningful possibility of a sympathetic or divinatory entry into the person of Christ, into his inner life (as W. Herrmann puts it).

Of the many epistemological problems which arise when we speak of understanding Christ, I will deal only with two, and those very briefly.

(1) Understanding, as we have seen, is tied to a certain analogy between the one who understands and what he understands. I can understand only that which belongs to my world. As Goethe put it, if the eye were not radiant, it could never see the sun. But I have to regard myself as one who has fallen away from the truth of God. How, then, can I understand the King of truth? No analogy exists to make this possible. The synoptic records are full of examples showing that Jesus was not known or understood. He was viewed as a rabbi, a wonder-worker, a man full of mana, a political messiah and much else. For people evaluated him by the analogies at their disposal and he did not fit these analogies. In particular the parables of Jesus, which make use of analogies to the familiar world of man and nature, prove almost as by an experiment that he transcends all the parallels we know and that hardness and misunderstanding are greatest where one would logically expect them to be dispelled (Matt. 13:13). He who is the truth is understandably not at the disposal of those who are not in the truth. Whether I can understand him who is the truth depends on whether he first brings me to the truth, or, epistemologically, on whether he sets up an analogy with himself. To that extent I am an object of calling. Only if there is calling first can Christ be an object of understanding for me. For only he who is of the truth, or who is brought to the truth, hears his voice.

(2) As one who is called I am claimed with my existence. What is engaged is not just my ear or perceptive reason but what the Bible calls my heart, my per-

sonal center. I am not just called to hear and think but to follow and to be in fellowship. But this means existential participation to a high degree. The goal is not simply to grasp the truth, but to be in the truth, that is, to exist in the name of the faithfulness of God which is bodily before me in Christ. Discipleship, then, cuts deep into my life. It means breaking with the past. It means changes and partings. I lay my hand to a plow which allows no looking back. All values are transvalued. I have to leave what is familiar and secure. I must even turn my back on what I previously regarded as a pious duty (Matt. 8:18-22).

### 4. The Special Nature of Theological Understanding

Since this calling by one who knows me before I can understand him (John 1:48) is an experience that is not at my command, and since the understanding of Christ is thus grounded in presuppositions which are not at my disposal, the mode of this understanding seems to be different from anything that we normally have in mind when we think of universities and faculties and when we consider the methods and concepts of science. For when we turn to theological understanding, two conditions seem to be missing which constitute the character of ordinary study and its understanding, first, that of universality, and second that of controllability. When the ability to understand is linked to a calling and the related existential presuppositions (namely, being in the truth), the constitutive criteria of all branches of knowledge seem to be lacking. Hence it may be seriously asked what a faculty of theology is doing in a university.

I believe I must try to make this clearer. The concept of knowledge on which the modern university rests is rational to the extent that its axioms are self-evident, that they rest on the *a priori* structure of our consciousness, and that the relation between them and the methods of research and constructs of thought is plain. To say this, however, is to say that the integration of theology into this structure of scholarship raises serious difficulties.

For theology implies the category of the revelation of truth. It involves encounter with something that no eye has seen or ear heard, as Paul puts it (1 Cor. 2:9). This something is not evident in principle. It cannot even be the object of a postulate. Naturally, then, one is inclined to assume that theology must be regarded as an alien body in the system of rational sciences. It introduces, as it were, non-planetary material into this system.

To measure the difference that exists here we need only point out how resolutely Kierkegaard viewed the Christian reality of salvation as wholly other, as a reality which is defined in a totally different way.

Kierkegaard's famous statement about the infinite qualitative distinction between time and eternity perhaps achieves its most forceful expression in the doctrine of the Holy Spirit. For this doctrine does not just say that the content of the Christian kerygma, namely, salvation history, breaks the continuity of the historical process and rests on a special or supernatural dispensation of the Lord of history. It also says that the historical content is accessible only in the form of a supernatural self-disclosure. According to the older tradition the idea of revelation does not mean only that something special has happened objectively. It also means that what has happened can be known only through a special form of illumination, namely, faith. This accessibility which is not at our disposal, the noetic side of the matter, has always been described as illumination by the Holy Spirit.

Paul describes this non-rational accessibility as follows. As the nature of man can be known only by man, so God alone can know what is in him (1 Cor. 2:11; cf. Thomas Aquinas, *Summa Theologiae* I, qu.12 a.4). Paul is alluding here to the necessary analogy between knower and known of which we spoke in point 3 above. We can know only that for which we are in some sense a match. I could never understand Plato's doctrine of the ideas

if Plato did not speak to certain analogous elements in my
consciousness, for example, the ability to form collective
concepts. In the case of God, however, nothing outside
him is equal to him or a match for him. Hence, he alone
can know himself. Only his own self-consciousness can be
in sympathy with him. This theological epistemology is
formally plain to everybody.

In development of it, the idea of revelation means
God's self-disclosure in the sense that he causes other
beings to share his self-consciousness and to understand
his truth. Hence, revelation is not exhausted by the popular idea of it as a form of supernatural inspiration. At
issue is a basic relation between God and men, namely,
that of the qualitative difference between them and God's
objective inaccessibility. The epistemological problem
based on this difference is described in the concept of
revelation. It is a problem which is overcome only by the
miracle of the divine self-disclosure, by God's enabling us
to share in his own self-knowledge.

Putting all this in a formula, we may advance the
thesis that the concept of revelation does not denote primarily a set of events, or, more crudely, the biblical
record, but in the epistemological sense a category, namely, a form of spiritual or religious experience. This form
is characterized by the fact that it brings us knowledge
only by participation in the divine self-knowledge. (Those
familiar with Pannenberg will see that we diverge from
him at this point.)

The object of Christian faith, then, is a circle
which is closed on all sides against the onrush of reflection. It is a circle of those called to discipleship. There are
no rational entrances into it by, for example, proofs of
God or apologetic bridges whose construction is motivated
by the ambition to give plausibility to the incomprehensi-
ble. Hence the inclusion of a theological faculty in the
organism of university disciplines does in fact raise a
problem, especially for theology's understanding of itself.

Does it not seem to bring into the sphere of the

rational sciences a heteronomous element in the sense that the general axioms of modern scholarship, which are all at our disposal, must yield here to a given authority which seems to set up in advance what is being sought, the result being that the circle of theological knowledge necessarily appears to be a vicious circle to those who share the normal concept of knowledge? At this point we seem to be confronted by the very opposite of what is called presuppositionless science.

On closer inspection the relation between theology and other university disciplines is seen to be a very complicated and dialectical relation of attraction and repulsion.

The theological faculty is in some sense a little university of its own and thus exerts the charm and causes the offense of an alter ego. All the themes and methodological problems of nearly all the academic disciplines crop up in it. Its biblical investigations use the methods of philology and hermeneutics. We find there all the problems of understanding which arise with historical texts and personal life. Church history involves all the problems of historical research and the philosophy of history. Systematic theology is in contact and tension with the material and methodological areas of philosophy. It runs parallel to this to the degree that philosophy leads to metaphysics and world views. In its own way it touches on the history of philosophy and the philosophy of history. It also raises epistemological problems in presenting a doctrine of the Fall and the healing of reason, of the transgressing of the limits of natural knowledge and the limitation of this knowledge. If time allowed, it could easily be shown that the presuppositions and themes of natural science are also dealt with in the process of theological thought, at least to the extent that they are relevant there.

All that takes place in theological research stands to other disciplines both methodologically and materially in a distinctive relation of analogy and distance, in a relation which has thus been described as one of both attraction and repulsion. The historian, the philosopher, and the philologist are all forced to exclaim: "This is flesh of our flesh and spirit of our spirit," while in the next breath offering the diagnosis: "It might also be a phantom, a forgery." The methods used agree with ours and yet they are handled in a special way, since they are applied to objects which necessarily appear to us to be beyond the grasp of understanding.

If the theologian were simply a variation of the religious man who appeals to ecstasies or to the mystical-theosophical knowledge of higher worlds, a tolerant irony might be exercised which is prepared to accept the freedom of fools. If constitution and temperament allow, there might also be a readiness to grant these colleagues at least the title of seriousness and to explain them in terms of a kind of typology: some men have a sixth sense or a special metaphysical sensitivity which must be treated with modest reserve by those who do not have it. A fugue by Bach can be acknowledged even when it is not understood.

The very fact, however, that theology claims to be a scientific undertaking makes this attempt at toleration difficult and constantly forces us to seek a point of intersection between the different lines of thought and of the sense of truth. For we are called and condemned to stand by the third thing which is above both. This third thing is the truth itself which necessarily overarches the two dimensions and which by nature can be only one. This means, however, that we have to put up with one another and remain open to opposing claims.

Theology must face up to the university and listen to it. It has to face up to the sense of truth in the university—the sense of truth which is inclined to accuse theology of heteronomy. The question which the university poses is whether the theological faculty is after all only a functionary of the church whose job it is with dialectical tools to deck out as science what is a fixed and predetermined ideology, to spruce up the old clothes, as

Goethe once put it. Along these lines theology has to take seriously the famous question of Rilke whether the orange has not been sucked dry, whether it is not trying to draw water from a well that two thousand years have exhausted. Thus the existence of the university puts a constant question to a theological faculty. Are its members ready to question their own principles before the truth with a free sense of responsibility that is independent of the tasks of the church? Even in their self-evident relation to the church are they prepared to serve, not as functionaries of the church, but as its free awareness of truth which is not subject to any commission?

At the same time the university must face up to its theological faculty. For the divinity department also has a question to put which represents a kind of threat to the general sense of truth and the monopoly of presuppositionless science. This question is as follows. Can there be a true criticism of reason, of the epistemological organ which conditions all knowledge, when reason itself is the instrument used, when the criticism is attempted with immanent means? Is not this completely impossible? Is it not conceivable that, as man cannot see himself but has a blind-spot in relation to self-knowledge, so reason cannot see itself or question itself but needs an external criterion by which to measure its powers and limitations?

In fact theology is speaking of such a suprarational criterion when it finds the destiny of reason bound up with the personal destiny of man himself and when it thus speaks of a fallen and hybrid reason which rationally validates man's fears and hopes, which sets up ideologies, and which fashions world views that are at man's command. Precisely in speaking of this reason which has become incurable and which ignores its own limits, theology recognizes on the other hand the fact that the event of redemption extends to the sphere of reason too.

In this sense there is a theological criticism of "impure" reason, a criticism which differs from Kant's epistemological criticism in virtue of the fact that it takes place on another level. For whereas Kant's criticism throws light on the structure of reason, its categorical functions, theological criticism begins with an investigation of the existence that encompasses reason, talking of the fall and rising again of this existence, and regarding reason as only one of the dimensions of human life which are totally and unreservedly bound up with the fate of man.

The secret of reason does not lie in itself or its functional structure. It is wholly human. Reason is human reason. There is thus a redeemed reason which is brought to itself and set again in its own order as redeemed and regenerate man is also reordered. Of this reason which is freed for God and for itself it may be said that the peace of God is higher than all reason but that under the peace of God reason is supreme.

In all this I am not trying to dramatize the tension between the sense of truth in the university and that in the theological faculty or to say that the feeling of being mutually threatened is the link between them. The drama of mutual challenge which may sometimes occur at high points in the dialogue or in hours of ultimate encounter is usually lightened in everyday academic life by another and very wholesome feeling, namely, that of human curiosity. This curiosity focuses on the way the other exists and thinks. I do not think I am being too partisan if I venture to say that in general theologians are amiable and cultivated persons who feel at home in many faculties and who carry—and settle—in themselves the problem of the double sense of truth.

Since both dimensions of the double sense of truth —which is naturally to be differentiated from so-called double truth—obviously occur in personal union in those who as believers have both a scholarly consciousness and also a love of methodologically purified knowledge, it must surely be possible, at least formally, to reach agreement on the methods of theological knowledge even with those who do not share the material presupposition of this knowledge, namely, the Christian faith. I should like to say a little more about this in the last section.

## 5. The Connection between the Object and Method of Knowledge

The method with whose help I know an object depends on this object. This principle is easily supported when we consider matters which can be approached from very different angles. Suicide, for example, is one subject for ethics and another for statistics.

For ethics, suicide is a matter of philosophical decision. This decision embraces many facets according to my understanding of existence. I stand before the question of whether I should destroy myself physically, that is, the question of life and death, of responsibility to the Creator, of the nexus of sin and guilt which I want to escape.

For statistics, however, suicide is simply a matter of figures. The individual instance is part of a graph which rises and falls annually and manifests a surprising constancy, so that it has almost the character of a law of nature. The suicide is thus dehumanized or dehistoricized; he is no more than a point on a graph. The elements of individual decision in all their multiplicity no longer play any decisive role.

Two conclusions follow.

First, I may view suicide either as a problem of human ethics or as a phenomenon of scientific law. The method I use to come to know it will depend on whether I characterize it as the one theme or the other.

Second, the reverse is also true. According to the method I use to know suicide, according to my choosing an ethical approach or a statistical approach, I shall have a basically different object in view.

The dialectic which rules here might be described in this way. The object determines the method and the method shapes the object. If I break the connection between the act of knowledge and the object, absurd results follow. To take an example, imagine a girl who is thinking of drowning herself because of an unhappy love affair letting her decision depend on whether there is a place free for her on the suicide graph. This statement is both macabre and comical. The comedy lies in the juxtaposition. Diametrically opposed objects, suicide understood ethically and suicide understood statistically, are mixed up no less than the approaches to them or the methods by which they are known.

Thus the objects of knowledge are profoundly ambivalent. They can be the objects of very different sciences and approaches. This ambivalence covers the objects of theology as well. Indeed, in this area it is particularly intense. In theology we thus see with special clarity a phenomenon which is familiar to us in other intellectual fields. A brief sketch of this will be given.

The heart of Christian proclamation is the Christmas message: "The Word was made flesh." This means that when we now say "God" in terms of this event, we can no longer think of a transcendence which is accessible only to mystical ecstasy or speculative flights. We have in view the God who moves history, who comes into it, and who accepts solidarity with man. This act of divine condescension into flesh or history, this downward movement, comes to expression in the temptation and passion of Christ, in which he surrenders all superiority to the world and thus makes intelligible the thesis of Luther that we cannot take God too deeply into the flesh.

If we take seriously this aspect of the Christian message, namely, that God became flesh, that the Lord of history became a figure in history, then the question arises how and in what sense this event of the Christmas miracle can be an object of knowledge for us. In other words, on what methodological presuppositions can there be an approximation of knowledge to this reality?

The only possible answer to this question is that fundamentally and continually this salvation event will have two aspects as elemental processes do in micro-physics. These aspects may be described as follows.

On the one side, the salvation event is part of earthly occurrence. It belongs to the history of religion. It can be documented as such and is thus a possible historical theme. It takes place within immanent reality. In this dimension the years A.D. 1-30 are obviously an object of secular history (cf. E. Norden, *Die Geburt des Kindes,* 1924).

On the other side, the true theme of this event, its character as the salvation event, is not exhausted when it is understood as part of history in general. For we have here a process in which the Lord of history becomes a figure in history. But only faith can know him as this Lord. Faith becomes here, as it were, a category of knowledge.

Once we realize that we really have here the salvation event, the self-disclosure of the personal God, this event, to be an object of knowledge, demands the personal category of faith.

Even in the human sphere there are some things which only the personal category of love can know. There are things for which love has the same epistemological function as faith has for the salvation event. For what is called objective, unprejudiced, and therefore loveless knowledge, things like nobility or even charm mean little. Goethe had this in view when he made his famous statement that we can understand only what we love.

It is true, then, that the salvation event belongs to the early history of Christianity, to what took place in A.D. 1-30. The Lord was born, crucified, and raised again at this time. In all these facts the salvation event was ontically there. But this does not mean that the salvation event is accessible in the same way as the historical facts with which it is connected. Kierkegaard can even say that by entering history Christ gave up ordinary knowability. He is not present, then, in the usual way. His historicity —to use what became a famous phrase—is a kind of incognito. For by entering the stream of religious history Christ exposes himself to ambivalence. He can be taken for an ordinary figure on the stage of history, for a founder of religion, or a religious man.

The difference between the two aspects does not have to mean that men are divided into two groups, one of which takes the objective historical approach and the other the existential approach of faith. The fact is that both aspects are present together in the believing Christian. For the Christian who has faith in the Kyrios Christos also sees him and the events relating to him as part of the stream of religious history. He is aware that Christ also has his place in intellectual processes. He recognizes analogies to other religions such as the Dionysus cult. In the coexistence of the two aspects he even finds theological meaning. For the ambivalence to which this gives rise is part of the nature of faith, faith being opposed to sight, to the grasping of what is directly before us. The ambivalence shows that the object of faith is not at our disposal. It discloses itself only in the gift of faith.

In a distinctive way, therefore, we find confirmation here of the epistemological thesis that the object of knowledge determines the category and methods by which we know it. The same fact—we think again of suicide—takes on a different quality when approached with the methods of ethics on the one hand or those of statistics on the other. The same is true, formally at least, when we are dealing with the fact which on the one side is a datable event of history but on the other side an incursion of eternity.

Hence one of the axioms of knowledge worked out and used especially in epistemology and hermeneutics is that in the act of understanding there must be a strict analogy between the knowing subject and the known object. We have already spoken of this, and in elucidation of the analogy have referred to some typical statements of Dilthey and Bultmann.

The decisive and disturbing problem regarding the relation between the university and the theological faculty is whether the analogy necessary for understanding is available when it is a matter of the divine realities and salvation events which theology describes as its truth. Here and here alone is the critical point in the so-called strife of the faculties. Theology says that naturally this analogy does not exist. Hence there is no such thing as natural theology. The fact that the analogy does not exist rests on the existential fate of man which the Christian message calls sin. Sin means the alienation of man from the Lord of his life and entails a breach of fellowship. This break in communication between God and man means epistemologically the loss of the analogy and consequently exclusion from the knowledge of God.

This gives us a new slant on the saying of Paul that no eye has seen, nor ear heard, nor has it entered the heart of man. We can now see the epistemological background of the saying. The point is that we are analogous to the historical facts of religious history, including those of Christianity, but we are not analogous to the divine truth which manifests itself in the facts of Christian history. Christ is incognito within the facts.

An important conclusion follows. If there is to be theological knowledge, an understanding of salvation events, the analogy must be restored in an act of new creation. The divine Word must create the hearer, the subject of understanding. The place in theology which deals with this creative function of the Word, this creation of the hearer, and the whole subject of theological epistemology, is the doctrine of the Holy Spirit. For this doctrine, as I have pointed out already, tells us that we are called to participation in the divine self-knowledge and that we are thus set in the true analogy. In this sense the Spirit (pneuma) searches all things, even the deep things of God (1 Cor. 2:10).

At the same time it is clear why theology can never call its epistemological processes heteronomous.

Heteronomy is present only when the object of faith, and hence of knowledge too, is dictated from outside, so that we have dogmas in the sense of obligatory propositions. For those who are called to the new analogy faith is not dictated; it is free and spontaneous. This faith, like love, is not commanded. It is won by the force of him who is encountered. What is spontaneity for faith is evidence in the epistemological act related to faith. But as this evidence is not at our command, theological utterances cannot have the character of demonstration or proof but only that of proclamation, address, and claim. These utterances are possible, however, only in trust in the awakening, creative, and efficacious power of the entrusted Word.

### 6. The Critical Significance of Theology

I may conclude with a question which theology as thus oriented has to put to the university.

This question is whether the university represents a closed truth or a truth which is open and ready to listen. Truths which are open to the hearer may be investigated at the level of their premises. Truths which are closed easily become ideologies. Whether in the form of church dogmatism, or in that of the dogmatism of the faculties of philosophy, law, and so forth, they give evidence of doctrinaire decay.

To return to Spengler's formulation, there are different "races" of dogmatism. Common to all of them, however, is the infusion of uncontrollable presuppositions and the acceptance of metaphysical hypostasizings, even when metaphysics is repudiated!

In face of this common factor no faculty is more critical, vigilant, and sceptical than the theological faculty. Its pharmacies are full of inoculations against latent ideologies. It reacts against these with allergic hyper-sensitivity.

The presence of a theological faculty means that a

question is constantly put to the ultimate presuppositions of all knowledge. And since the final thing in knowledge is not a truth which is valid but a truth in which one *is*, this question is in the last resort addressed to searching man himself and his existence. When the New Testament says that he who is of the truth hears my voice, this lets out the secret that ultimately truth is not an object of knowledge but a personal state. This truth is the actual relation, disclosed in faith, with him who is the truth. We are already grasped by him and we are waiting to grasp his truth. We are already known by him and we are waiting to know him and to see him as he is (1 John 3:2). We wait for the eschaton of truth.

If the theological faculty is perhaps in some sense the conscience of the university, the voice of this conscience summons us not merely to seek the truth ahead of us (in possible objects of knowledge) but also to seek it behind us (in the truth of our being into which we are called and from which the acts of our knowledge proceed).

In this way, perhaps, the theological faculty can be a thorn in the flesh of the university, or, better, gauze in the wound of our existence, the wound caused by the mysterious spear of being which challenges us and demands *aletheia*, unveiling. This wound must not heal too quickly. The smooth skin which closes over it may be deceptive. The university must never be closed. Its knowledge must progress and those who know must always be ready for revisions. Hence the theological faculty can serve as gauze in the wound.

# V

# The Question of God

## 1. What Is Meant by the Word God: The Modern Crisis in the Concept of God

What does it mean to talk about God? A common answer today is that it means nothing. Theism has become a term of reproach in theology. There are no bars against revelation, especially when material statements are in view. These cause no embarrassment, so long as they carry a message and are relevant. Existential or ethical criteria of relevance may even be accepted. But if a revelation or kerygma rests on the evidence of what it says, there is no need to ask about the author. In relation to the Pythagorean theorem, Pythagoras is of little interest. Concentration on what is relevant, or self-evident, makes the question of the author unnecessary. Indeed, the question of the author might indicate the need for a guarantee, as though one's own criteria and judgments were not enough and authoritarian support were needed. God or a god must be sought so as to give the certainty of a "God said" to what is uncertain. Resort to metaphysical supports of this kind is regarded as a sign of immaturity.

We thus reach the situation where a theology calling itself Christian could speak of the death of God without feeling that this was a declaration of bankruptcy but rather with the feeling of liberation for adult confrontation with what is at issue in the supposed "God said." The belief was that this thing at issue could stand on its own feet, and on the insight it gives, without having to be validated by a "God said."

But the questioning of God involves more than the argument that the kerygma can stand alone without any inquiry as to its author and without any divine guarantees. This argument links up with some general tendencies in the scientific and philosophical world.

Science, like other spheres ruled by immanent autonomies such as politics and economics, does not need the God hypothesis (Laplace). It rules out in principle transcendent interventions and the author of such interventions. Even in religious or broader philosophical circles the concept of God has ceased to be self-evident as earlier epochs thought it to be. God the almighty "who o'er all things so wondrously reigneth" but inactively watches the sufferings of the innocent is called in question. Camus expresses the corresponding reaction very accurately in his idea of the absurd.

We thus face a distinctive reversal of previous questionings.

Earlier the existence of God was taken for granted but doubt arose as to the validity and function of Christ. But today the reverse is often true. Christ is accepted as a paradigm of man's finite and questionable existence, but God is set in the dubious light of a theistic preamble (H. Braun). Hence, the question arises with mounting urgency what it can mean to talk about God, especially as the subject of revelation.

This secular and theological questioning of God does not have to lead to radical atheism. As often happens in the church, the word "God" may be kept, but under its cover a shift of meaning takes place. God is regarded as a cipher for something else. This something else which he first mediates will finally replace him. Thus God is for Kant a description of the unconditional validity of moral commands.

It almost has the rank of a thesis that when God

is a cipher for something other than himself he becomes
superfluous and yields to that other. If the word "God"
means only what the world is in principle saying to itself,
if it is merely a propaedeutic description of this, then it
means nothing.

Two questions arise in this regard. The first is
this: What is the distinctive element in God which cannot be identified with anything else, even with being
itself in Tillich's sense, and which blocks the inter-
changeability of the concept of God with any other
concept?

Second, what is the proper course between the
Charybdis where God means something, but can be detached from what is meant, and the Scylla where he is
simply said to exist in doctrinaire fashion?

These are the questions we must now try to
answer.

The scientific atheism which rejects transcendent
guidance and intervention in principle, and substitutes
the premise of a closed world immanence, has been reduced to a famous formula by Bonhoeffer: It cannot
accept a God of the gaps. To pursue apologetics along
the old lines of a God of the gaps is to condemn belief in
God to a lingering death. For the boundaries of knowledge will be continually extended. God will be in continual
retreat. Instead, says Bonhoeffer, God is to be sought in
what is known, not in what is not known, in solved questions, not in unsolved questions. Now that man has come
of age, God must be rethought on the premise of man's
autonomy and related to the new situation. It is absurd to
try to prove to an adult world that it cannot live without
God's tutelage. It has already shown that it can. The
attempt to prove the opposite is reactionary. It resembles
a foolish attempt to put an adult back in the stage of
puberty.

The negative side of Bonhoeffer's case, his attack
on the seeking of God in the realm of ignorance and on
the margin of experience, is helpful. But the positive

implications are unclear and this allows full play for interpreters. What does it mean to seek God in what is known? What does it mean to approach the biblical data on the basis of man's adulthood and to subject them to secular interpretation? How, positively, can God be known afresh in the new situation? We thus come back to the original question. What does it mean to talk about God? What content does the word have?

In the previous century apologetics was not prepared to accept the scientific idea of a closed universe. It thus tried to find gaps and discontinuities where God could be seen at work. Today the situation has changed fundamentally. Hence Bonhoeffer is simply formulating the theological understanding of many before and after him and what might almost be called the common view of our age.

In contrast to the 19th century view, self-resting finitude (as Tillich calls it) is now the starting-point of almost all theological reflection in biblical studies and also in dogmatics and ethics. There is no point, then, in contesting the heuristic principle of all scholarship or breaking the cosmic nexus to find a place for God. Gogarten has even argued that Christianity itself has authored secularization and the thesis of closed immanence.

Contesting the same apologetic attempt to find a hint of God or a place for God in immanence, Karl Barth has rejected any point of contact for faith in the natural man. In his *Romans* he argued already that any talk of God outside Christian proclamation is a dubious form of religion, that is, human self-deification. When the Christian message is proclaimed, Godless man, enclosed in his immanence, is addressed. Hence there is no apologetic porch where arguments can first be used to breach this immanence and thus create the conditions of an ability to hear.

In Bultmann's hermeneutics the modern scientific and historical presupposition of immanence is the decisive theological premise. It provides a ready criterion for distinguishing between what is kerygmatically relevant and what is culturally conditioned, namely, what speaks of transcendent and mythical interventions and miracles. Rejection of the attempt to find God and his revelation in historical immanence has for Bultmann two results. The first is indifference to the facticity of what is recorded, so that critical eliminations do not affect kerygma-faith. The second is that insistence on the truth of the records is an illegitimate prop for faith.

Similarly G. Ebeling thinks that historical research (based on the principle of immanence) should shatter the supposed historical certainties which make the decision of faith unnecessary. The Reformation doctrine of justification must be applied here too. In relation to history the Yes to uncertainty is simply the reverse side of the certainty of salvation by faith alone (*Word and Faith*, 1963, pp. 1ff.). It is highly paradoxical that, in contrast to all other research, the aim in this research is to become uncertain.

Even if faith is so unsettled that it regards any historical support for its object as an illegitimate support and to that extent as unbelief, the trend shows how radical is the departure from earlier apologetics. God is no longer confined to laboriously discovered lacunae and discontinuities in researchable immanence. No places are found for him in the world. The closed nexus is accepted in the sense of the working hypothesis of science and the modern experience of life. It is made the starting-point of theology. Modified thus, the question of God asks whether and how far what is attested about God in the Bible applies unconditionally to the man enclosed in immanence, whether and how far it changes his existence, calls him to decision, and qualifies his existence afresh.

But can the absolute paradox of non-demonstrability really be a basis of faith? Does not faith become here a leap into the void under attraction from an unknown source? Even if I do hear from the historical no-

man's-land a voice which cannot be identified in time
or space but which summons me and unconditionally
applies to me, might it not be that what I receive is
simply secular existentialism or a Socratic appeal, so that
it, too, is an element in immanence and can be integrated
into this? And if so, does it matter what voice speaks, or
whether it really speaks at all? Possibly what the voice
says is simply what man is saying to himself. Does faith
really have to have a basis (a foundation, not a cause)
which makes it a decision for the scandal that is outside
everything that relates to man in his immanence? For
many things do relate to him here too: the link between
the generations, the love of the sexes, hunger and anxiety,
hope and longing, threats and natural gifts, human communication and human enmity, the justice and injustice
of historical structures, and much else. Does that which
is unconditionally relevant to me have to be without relation to what is conditionally relevant to me? Does not
this involve a new docetism, a mere appearance of
bodiliness, which supposedly relates to me kerygmatically
but summons me away from all relation to immanent
reality? Is not this an absolute non-historicity which reduces man to immanent and even solipsistic existence and
thus makes the question of God irrelevant in respect of
the involvement of existence in natural bios and historical
structures?

One thing may be affirmed. The question of God
is relevant only if the God who relates to me unconditionally is seen in some connection with that which relates
to me conditionally. Whether there is an analogy between
these two forms of relating, whether the unconditional
form is quantitatively higher than the conditional, or
qualitatively different from it and perhaps totally other,
may be left open for the moment. The important point
here is that there has to be a connection between them if
God is not to sink into docetic irrelevance. The protest
against a theism which makes God so otherworldly that
he has no contact with this world, which views him as a

doctrinaire authority and not the basis of a conviction, is right on its negative side, that is, in its criticism of the discontinuity of this God with the phenomena of immanence. But to go on to speak of the death of God or his total irrelevance is to go too far. Only the God of this kind of theism is dead. Only a dubious concept of God dies.

The concept that there must be a connection between the unconditional and the conditional relation if the relevance of God is to be credible comes to expression in Tillich's principle of correlation. But here the connection is limited by the ontology of Tillich. Thus God is the infinite power of being when seen in correlation with the threat that non-being poses to existence. He is the ground of courage when related to anxiety as awareness of finitude. Tillich's concern is to show how the concept of God is so actualized for us that it relates to us and is no mere assertion. But is it enough when the actualizing connection is limited to such existential things as anxiety, threat, and the sense of absurdity? Should it not be extended to historical structures such as politics or economics if God, or the concept of God, is to relate to man in the complex concreteness of his existence and not just his inner life?

In this sense it has to be possible to discuss "theo"-logically the problems of organ transplants, artificial prolongation of life, political protest, capital punishment, partnership in industry, and social systems, showing that the question of God applies in these areas too. If it cannot be demonstrated that historical structures have a human center, and that human existence as thus structured experiences the question of God in every dimension, then we are still under the spell of theistic docetism.

But how are we to make this relevance of God clear without demanding a theologizing of the sciences and historical structures and foolishly trying to reverse the universal secular axiom according to which the knowledge and control of the world must be on the basis of self-enclosed immanence? If we avoid this route, what does it mean to speak of the relevance or actuality of the idea of God?

We are thus brought back to our original question. What does it mean, under these conditions, to talk about God?

No one really disputes the thesis that the concept of God can be relevant only in connection with other actualities, even though recognition of it may be very general or under existential restriction. Emil Brunner has it in mind in his point of contact, Althaus in his primal revelation, Bultmann in his pre-understanding, and even Barth, in whom one would least expect it, points to connections of this kind in his *Epistle to the Romans* (cf. W. Pannenberg, *Grundfragen der systematischen Theologie*, 1967, pp. 366f.).

## 2. Negative and Positive Aspects of the Concept of God

(1) The question of God is wrongly put if couched in terms of traditional theism. In this case God is already presupposed. It is simply a matter of what we should believe about him. There is no individual encounter, no hearing or experiencing of God's self-declaration. One simply adopts in answer to the theistic question of God the description which is nearest to hand. Christian tradition and environment are the sources. We thus have a host of fellow-travellers, of nominal Christians who have gone through the rite of baptism. Discipleship is simply conformity to the traditional trend according to the law of least resistance. It is quickly abandoned if the wind shifts. Or it might rest on a pragmatism which irrespective of the question of God thinks it useful to respect religious beliefs and practices. Power can be gained in this way. Others are made docile by religious observance. Religion is good for the nation.

The basis of the pragmatic and conformist misunderstanding of the question of God is that the question has no existential application, and the less so the more its purpose is perceived (cf. Feuerbach, Nietzsche, and Marx). It can thus be manipulated pragmatically and becomes increasingly unworthy of belief. The role of the church in secularized society offers a grim example of this.

(2) The question of God is wrongly put if it does not carry with it questions that concern us, for example, when it is simply a matter of how to find a gracious God or arises out of other experiences of reality that are no longer our own.

This may be seen in the orthodox doctrine of general revelation. The modern experience of reality reflected in philosophy and poetry is far too ambivalent, far too drastically marked by a sense of the absurd, to be ready or able to detect and recognize traces of God in nature and history. Thus Camus has the physician Rieux say that he cannot forgive God for letting innocent children suffer. The death-of-God conclusion that we can no longer after Auschwitz sing of the God "who so wondrously reigneth," misguided though it may be, is rooted in the experience of this absence, this lack of any trace of God. When, in spite of this, faith in God persists, and looking back finds traces of God by the analogy of faith, it is always grounded in original encounters and does not rest on a preceding experience of reality in the sense of traces or evident proofs of God. Extreme experiences may actualize the theme of the God question. But because of their ambivalence they can just as well lead to rejection instead of acceptance, to cursing or sheer indifference instead of to prayer.

When we said above that if the relevance of God is to be seen there has to be a connection between the conditionally and the unconditionally relevant, this correspondence does not mean that there has to be a kind of natural theology or a reaching of God by deduction from our relation to reality. Faith is not just faith *in*; it is also faith *against*. Faith defies the elements in natural experience that seem to rule out God. Thus the problem of theodicy discussed in Psalms 73 and 77 is closer to today's experience of reality and to modern God-movements than is the natural theology of orthodoxy.

(3) The question of God is wrongly put if God is identified as the ground of a dimension of being, for example, the author of divine commands (Kant) or a symbol of the unconditional nature of moral duty. For in such cases he can claim only interim validity, which stands opposed to his majesty. A dawning sense of autonomy makes him superfluous. The same applies when he is regarded as the basis of utopian hope (Bloch) or the fulfilment and unity of history (Tillich).

Whenever the unconditional is fused with a conditional, no matter how highly qualified the latter may be, the conditional will break free as an idea which can be viewed as self-conceived and thus interpreted atheistically, that is, without any help from the God-hypothesis. A vacuum is thus left (Bloch). God, in distinction from the mere God-hypothesis, obviously transcends the possibilities of a religion which results from the sacral and numinous transfiguring of areas of life. When a creature is identified as the Creator, not God is in view but an idol representing deified reality. But the idol passes into the twilight when the specific force of the deified dimension of reality is perceived and it shows itself to be something that stands in its own immanent power and needs no numinous transfiguring. Apollo has to vanish from the scene when the knowledge and wisdom he is supposed to impart become autarchous. The Delphic oracle is not needed when the future can be calculated by rational means.

(4) The question of God is wrongly put when the question of God enclosed in human existence is changed into an answer (cf. Rom. 1:18ff.). The question of God enclosed in human existence means that man himself becomes an open question. He sees himself always confronted by the problem of what he has been thrust into,

what will become of him, and what he is to make of himself. Unlike an animal, man is not a being whose entelechy unfolds autonomously from within itself (cf. Schiller's *Anmut und Würde,* 1793). He has to ask about his destiny. He has to ask about himself. He must venture an answer and may fail to achieve it (cf. Heidegger's *Being and Time*). Man, then, is an open possibility. Fulfilling the possibility is not present in a given form. Identity is not present in such a way that it can be read off from what he is now (cf. Max Frisch).

The same applies to the race. The goal of hope in which it reaches identity with its destiny is not the same as either present achievement or a utopian future. What has been or can be achieved can be excelled in principle, as can any utopia, even the classless society (Bloch, *Prinzip Hoffnung,* pp. 1410-13). In principle, then, man reaches beyond what he has become and is. His identity is hope and he is constantly reaching after it. The not-yet of man shows that he essentially transcends himself.

If God is regarded as the *locum tenens* of this transcendence—and we may say, provisionally and very formally, that Christian proclamation sees him within this framework—this means that he encounters us in our "natural" consciousness as the object of the question about ourselves and the basis of the investigation of what we are. Thus if God truly encounters us in his self-manifestation, he discloses the questionability of our being (Karl Barth, *Christliche Dogmatik,* 1927, p. 74), radicalizes it in the law, and declares that he is the answer to it. Since, however, God is not just a cipher for the question and answer which we are, since he does not arise merely as the postulate of an answer—such a postulate would always be preformed by the question—since he discovers and radicalizes the question as we could not do, the question which we are asking is always an open one within our natural horizon. It is even a question which we do not fully perceive, whose basis is hidden from us. The answer, which God is, forms the basis of the question.

The question of God is wrongly put, then, if it thinks it can itself give the answer, if with this answer it forestalls its own radicalization, if it remains a purely provisional and conditioned question. Paul interprets idolatry along these lines in Romans 1:18ff.

God is manifest to the consciousness of pagans. He is the object of the question enclosed in the works of creation (v. 20), including man himself. But this question does not remain an open one. It is answered too quickly. Its depth cannot be explored. The creature man does not stay with what transcends and questions him. He is not ready to see himself in his creatureliness. He refuses to give God praise and thanks (v. 21). He will not acknowledge the one from whom he has his identity and who gives him his destiny, from whom and to whom he is. Instead he isolates himself and curves in upon himself. The question which he himself is offers its own answer. This answer is not God but the idol, the likeness (v. 23) and magnifying of the creaturely in the form of winged, four-footed, and crawling creatures. He does not expect an answer which will transcend his question and his questionability, which might surprise him as something unexpected, as the wholly other, which he could not give himself, and which will cause him to see himself in a new light. He gives himself the answer and it is an answer which keeps him safely in his present existence, his old existence. God does not reach him with the counterquestion: "Where art thou, Adam?"—the question which radicalizes his questionability, which in the light of the answer discloses its basis. God reaches him in masked form as an idol, a bit of his own creatureliness, which keeps him safely and securely where he is.

God himself, however, remains outside this creature-idol relation. He does not enter it. The religion it founds is one that forgets the question which the true God puts to human existence and which is falsified when man gives the answer he wants. Thus man misses the point, namely, that it was meant to show him the basis of his questionability and thus give him the answer present already in the basis. Instead, man closes himself up. He wants to be alone with himself and creation. He does not want the question to be a questioning. He does not want to be confronted by the living God who as Creator has given him existence and who has a total claim upon him. Deified creatures do not question him. They are flesh of his flesh and spirit of his spirit. The identical cannot call itself in question. Command and judgment can come only from the outside, the transcendent. To this, then, man refuses praise and thanks. He thus negates it as that which is above himself and everything creaturely.

God himself also remains outside the creature-idol relation in the sense that when man falsifies his questionability God gives him up (*paredoken*, vv. 24, 26) to his decision. He leaves him to the consequences of the falsified question. He surrenders him to the fateful answer by which he obscures the openness of the question (vv. 24ff.). Perversion of the vertical relation, which brings about confusion of creature and Creator, leads to perversion of the horizontal relation. The orders of the world become chaotic when they rest in themselves and are detached from the transcendental basis which sustains them.

Thus God is the answer to the falsified question even when he gives man up and withdraws or retires (Léon Bloy). He is the answer in the form of the God of wrath. He retains sovereignty over those whom he silently gives up. He is still in control of what he permits. He still gives it its meaning and answer, namely, the meaning and answer of judgment. God remains outside the creature-idol relation by overruling it as Lord and Judge and by thus transcending it.

God is fundamentally the answer to the question enclosed in human existence. He is not identical with the answer man himself gives, no matter how pious or religious. Such an answer conceals man's real questionability and stops the openness for which he is destined. It thus intensifies, as one might say, the transcendence of God. This becomes a withdrawing transcendence which is no longer manifest to man or proffered to him (v. 19).

The question of God is wrongly put here to the extent that enclosed in human existence it is changed into an answer and is thus suppressed as a mere question.

It is perhaps the theological merit of Camus that he tried to stay in openness without an answer and preferred absurdity to snatching at a supposed answer. Is Camus the only one to have broken human solidarity here and thus to have escaped the verdict of Romans 1:18ff.? Might it not be that the original necessity of absurdity has surreptitiously become a virtue, a new discovery of meaning in the negative mode? Might it not be that Camus has come up with an answer in this highly dialectical fashion? Does absurdity really remain an open question in him? This line of thought is permissible, perhaps, as an expression of uncertainty.

We now turn to the positive aspect.

This aspect, and with it the legitimate question of God, arises when understanding of what is meant by the word "God" is related to the realities and indeed to the deficient aspects of human existence but also transcends them. Refusal to let the reality that is meant by God be restricted to immanent relations is affirmed even by the Roman Catholic doctrine of the analogy of being, for the Fourth Lateran Council points out (Denzinger, 432) that in the relation between Creator and creature the element of unlikeness or transcendence always outweighs that of likeness.

Since there can be no thoroughgoing analogy between the question of the unconditioned enclosed in human existence and the answer described by the word "God," it is impossible to equate God with answers whose material lies in creaturely relations. This is to absolutize the similitude and to make God a cipher for what the creature can itself deduce from the immanent reference.

We must now show from some examples why the reality we call God transcends all immanent relations, cannot be identical with them, and in distinction from them is non-objectifiable.

### (1) *God and Meaning*

If one asks about God expecting to find in him the point where the riddles, contradictions, and the whole meaning-lessness of history and our own existence are solved, it is a mistake to see in God merely the meaning that is sought and in his kingdom merely a representation of the unity and coincidence of historical processes, that is, the being that embraces all divergent being. This unity may be con-ceived of as an idea (cf. Hegel's reason in history). I can even make this idea of unity the historical point from which to view history and try to master the empirical with its help. These ideas, of course, cannot be proved empirically. They are categorial functions of the mind. Or, like Kant's highest good, they are the object of eschatological hope. But this does not prevent them from being related to the autarchy of reason, so that God is not needed. If the term "God" means something specific and is not just a synonym for the unity and basis of meaning of history, this simply means that, although he is these too, he is also more and different. He is not exhausted in them.

But what is this extra element and how is it relevant? How am I to see that it is more than a mythi-cal husk whose kernel is the idea and which can be peeled off when reason grasps this? What is the extra element in the reality we call God?

The idea of the unity and the basis of meaning of history, whether we view it as a regulative idea of reason or as a social utopia such as the classless society, takes from man his non-definability. When I define the unity of history I deny the openness of historical possibility and make man the bearer of a necessary and definable func-tion in the historical process. Man no longer grasps him-self. He is grasped by the goal of history. He does not de-cide and come to himself in decision; decision is made over his head. He knows who he is and who he will be. His freedom (as in Hegel and Marx) is no more than insight into this necessity. One might also say that he is depersonalized. For the concept of person represents the openness of human possibility, the destiny of man to grasp his freedom.

We are thus caught on the horns of a dilemma. On the one hand, to be able to exist historically, we have to ask about the unity and meaning of history so as to be able to orient and shape ourselves and not be given up to a chaotic and shapeless web in which we are merely pushed about as objects (cf. Thedor Lessing, *Die Geschichte als Sinngebung des Sinnlosen*, 1927). On the other hand, answering this question robs us of the presuppositions of the question itself, namely, the possibility of understanding human existence as open, personal, and faced with decision.

Precisely that in the word "God" which goes beyond the unity and meaning of history and cannot be enclosed in these concepts opens our eyes to a meaning of history which does not reduce us to an impersonal function but preserves the open and unconditional nature of our existence.

We are not definable inasmuch as the world does not know us, since it does not know God (1 John 3:1). We exist as a relation to God. For this reason we are no more definable than God. Only God defines us. We are known in him (1 Cor. 13:12). Because of this it does not yet appear what we shall be (1 John 3:2). Our life is now hidden with Christ in God. When Christ shall be manifested as our life, then we shall be revealed in glory with him (Col. 3:4; cf. Phil. 3:21). The fact that what we shall be is not yet seen, that the goal of the present is still concealed, shows that we stand before an open possibility, that we are not defined by the necessity of a process in which we are mere elements and functions, that we are not robbed of our openness. The relation that defines us is not an immanent one, whether to nature above which we lift ourselves, or to society of which we are to be useful members, or to an idea which we burn ourselves up in realizing. All these relations make us a function, a means to some other end. They thus take away our unconditionality. This unconditionality is kept only when man is related to an unconditioned which transcends immanent relations even though present in them and sustaining them. Only in relation to the unconditioned which we call God does human existence take on what Kierkegaard calls infinite reality.

Caution is needed here. The concept of the unconditioned which is meant to free God from immanent relations while maintaining correlation with all of them might itself become a synonym for God, taking up this term into itself and becoming interchangeable with it. In this case "God" would again be what Pascal calls the God of the philosophers, the logos structure of the cosmic nexus which sustains and determines all occurrence as its basis of unity, but is itself unconditioned. We would thus be overtaken by the same calamity as we noted earlier. The idea of "God" would merge into that of something else, the unconditioned, and might well be dissolved in it.

But the statement that it is not yet manifest what we shall be contains the antidote to this merging of God with the philosophical idea of the world logos or the unconditioned. It does so in two ways.

First, the unconditioned (in the masculine, not the neuter) knows who we are. He is not a postulate of ours. He first conceives of us and knows us. He knows us in love. He is open to us in freedom. Unlike the God of the philosophers, he is not just the unconditioned world logos who sustains the cosmic nexus and functions as the coincidence of opposites. He is understanding, love, and freedom. He confronts us as a person. This means that when we say "God" we say more than the unconditioned (in the neuter). God as the unconditioned does not reduce creaturely existence to the mere conditioned. He grants it the dignity of partnership. He who loves creates his image (Gen. 1:26f.), his counterpart. Whereas stars, plants, and animals are simply objects of a "Let there be," man is summoned to the freedom of partnership. He is addressed with a "Thou." He is given commands and goals (Gen. 1:28f.; 3:3, 9). He is made a subject who can decide between obedience and disobedience, who can stay in covenant with God or break the covenant, who can fulfil his destiny or fail to do so.

If God is understanding, love, and freedom, the basis of the world is not an abstract unconditioned but a person who grants personhood, who does not just condition but wants unconditionality, who does not integrate man into the cosmic nexus but calls him and grants him the privilege of immediacy which the God of the philosophers denies, replacing it with the mediacy of an assigned function.

That which we have called the transcendent element in the word "God," and that in which it is no mere synonym for the unconditioned, means that we can see in the word the coincidence of opposites which autonomous thinking would view as irreconcilable. For on the one hand we are understanding God as the meaning and unity of the world process but on the other hand we are understanding him as the one who upholds the openness of human existence. It does not yet appear what we shall be but we shall know it as we are known by him.

Secondly, if the word "God" means that the basis of the world is understanding, love, and freedom, this means that although the meaning and unity of the world process are found in God (so that he is in fact the point where opposites converge, and hence unconditioned), they cannot be objectified in a cosmic formula, so that what is and what happens, as they concretely encounter me, cannot be interpreted in terms of a formula of this kind. The mark of the biblical experience of God and the world lies precisely here. Job in his suffering fails in his attempt to find such a formula and to live and think on the premise that there is a just world order and that doing

right will finally pay off (Job 1:8ff.). Nor can the poet
of Psalm 73 understand the contradictions of world events
when he sees the wicked triumphing and the righteous
going under. Finding no formula, and therefore finding
no God if he is identified with such a formula, man concludes that the course of the world is absurd and meaningless, or at least inscrutable. Yet in spite of this, and
in spite of the fact that knowledge seems to be un-
attainable, the meaningfulness of the basis of the world
is not disputed. The noetic renunciation of knowledge goes
hand in hand with the confession of faith that ontically
there is meaning in the world. Even if he cannot subsume
what happens under a cosmic formula, the believer confesses: "Nevertheless I am continually with thee" (Ps.
73:23).

How is the gap to be filled?

If the background of the world that we call God is
understanding, love, and freedom, here and in him is
knowledge of meaning. As we are known in him, so is
meaning. We ourselves do not know it. Those who think
they do, lose the personal element in the ineluctability
of processes. But we believe in him who does know
meaning.

This does not simply imply that we replace knowledge of meaning by mere faith in meaning. If this were
so, faith would be a first stage of knowledge that we
could never get beyond. It would not be trust, but con-
jecture and defective knowledge. When we say God, we
stand to him, as the one who understands and loves, in a
relation of trust, and this trust implies certainty that
knowledge of the meaning unknown to us lies hid and
protected in him. The one who understands and loves is
the one who calls what is not into being (Rom. 4:17).
He thus gives shape to his thoughts in it. Since these
thoughts are his and not ours, and since they are higher
than ours (Isa. 55:8), we trust that they are thoughts—
not nonsense—and that they rule the world, even if they
are not our thoughts. Along these lines there is no reason

in history if what is meant by this is that our reason participates in it or that the finite spirit knows its knowledge as the absolute spirit (Hegel). It is another who knows and thinks here. Hence we can have access to this knowledge and thought only by way of trust in their subject, in this other.

It might be objected that this interpretation of the word "God" is merely an attempt to overcome a difficulty of thought with the help of more or less refined speculation. We are referring to the difficulty that we have to put the question of unity and meaning for the sake of our personhood but that we destroy this personhood when we find an answer in the form of a cosmic formula, whether it be materialistic or idealistic. Might it not be that this concept of God is just a speculative attempt to reconcile what seems to be irreconcilable?

This objection would find support if the idea of God arose simply as a construction of thought in the effort to interpret the world or human existence. Such an effort could lead only to the God of the philosophers, to the God who does not transcend the idea of a world basis but is exhausted in this idea. In contrast, our own attempt to interpret God in terms of the meaning and unity of world occurrence is undertaken in relation to the God of the Bible who basically transcends that idea.

We describe God in terms of love and freedom precisely in order to distinguish him from the God of the philosophers. Hence this God does not arise as a regulative idea in interpretation of the world. But how then do we come to faith in this God?

Our provisional answer—we shall have to be more precise when we speak of the name and person of God—is as follows.

This faith arises through the immediacy and demonstration of the self-disclosure that we call revelation. God makes himself known in his glory (Exod. 33:12ff.). He presents himself and his name at the burning bush (Exod. 3:13ff.). He appears in Christ and makes him his mirror (Luther). If always in the Bible this God discloses himself as the one who addresses the world and man in every dimension, it is on the basis of this encounter. All reflections with whose help events and personal existence are interpreted in this light (cf. Ps. 36:10) are triggered by this encounter and are emphatically subject to it. Israel understands its history, then, as a series of experiences of God. In the perplexities of the present it recalls his mighty works (Ps. 77:12). When things are inscrutable it takes comfort in past guidance. What cannot be understood for the moment becomes plain in retrospect (John 12:16). "Afterward you will understand" (John 13:7).

Faith, then, leads to understanding. It gives knowledge of the world even if the fact that God's thoughts are higher prevents a full theological interpretation or the reducing of those thoughts to our thoughts. When the world and history are understood in this way, there is no unriddling with the help of a concept of God misused as a cosmic formula. No, when this understanding is achieved, we have only signs and signals that are given to us. Only in the sanctuary does the Psalmist begin to see that the distribution of rewards and punishments in the world is not wholly inscrutable but that there are in it intimations of God's judgments (Ps. 73:17ff.; Jer. 2:19) or signs of a divine purpose (John 9:1ff.).

If we ask how inferences can be made here, we can only answer that they must not be made in the style of natural theology. We cannot work back from nature and history to God. Inferences can be made only from an encounter with the self-disclosing God and in the light of this encounter. From this alone can we understand the world that God has made and governs, its order and disorder, the nexus of guilt and destiny, the rule of Cyrus, Nebuchadnezzar, and others. Only along these lines is the question urgent why the reality we call God cannot be identical with the idea of something immanent in the world and why that in God which is above all that is and is accepted makes it possible for us to overcome the difficulty of thought to which we referred, namely, to think of the unity and meaningfulness of world processes without destroying the personal, unconditional, and subjective element in human existence. Our formula is: We do not know meaning but believe in him who does. We do not believe in him because we have found a speculative solution in some cosmic interpretation. We believe in him because he has made himself known and in the light of this we see the world with new eyes.

### (2) *God and the Good*

When it is a question of the good, too, the answer cannot be that God is a mere synonym for the good. Here again there is a transcendent element which the concept of the good does not possess.

In Matthew's version the rich young ruler puts to Jesus the question of the good: "What good thing shall I do to have eternal life?" (Matt. 19:16). The answer is: "Why do you ask me about the good? One alone is good" (v. 17; cf. Mark 10:18; Luke 18:19). Does this mean that God is the answer to the question of the good, that he is no more than the good thing the ruler is asking about, so that what he is really asking about is God? Is God a personification—or mythicization—of the norm of the good?

If so, then he can be replaced by this norm once man can grasp it autonomously. In this story, however, God is more and other than a mere norm of the good. The text points to the distinction in two essential nuances.

First, God is not called the good in the neuter. He is the good one in a personal sense. The good here is an attribute and it belongs to him alone: Only one is good. This means that the good does not exist in abstraction from him and that it may not be known apart from him. It cannot be defined as a generally valid and accessible norm but only in connection with the person of God. God, however, is not generally accessible. He has to make himself known (Isa. 29:14; Matt. 11:25ff.; Luke 10:21; John 17:25; 18:37). By nature, then, we do not know the good. It is disclosed to us only in the self-disclosure of God.

The second nuance is related to this. If the good can be essentially defined only in terms of the person with whom it is constitutively bound up, one can no longer say that God is good because he conforms to a prior norm of the good which can be known apart from him. What is good is essentially defined by God himself. It is characterized as the good personally, not neutrally. In illustration of what the good means, one may think of God's self-emptying, of his love, of his being for man (John 3:16; Rom. 5:8; 8:32; 1 John 4:9).

This reversal of the direction of definition corresponds exactly to what we find in John's Gospel on the one side and the Apologists on the other in relation to the Logos. For the Apologists, the Logos pervades all being and may be known by the philosopher. Christ represents this and is validated by the fact that he does. He is the Son of the God of the philosophers and may be known by speculative reason in the same way as the cosmic Logos. John, however, does not define Christ by the Logos. He defines the Logos by Christ. The Logos is the Word spoken by God and incarnate in Christ (John 1:1ff.). The Logos is bound to Christ once and for all. He is present only in him. He may be known only through his self-disclosure. Christ defines who (not what) the Logos is. More precisely the Logos is defined by the incarnate Logos in whom God discloses himself and is present. What is here true of the Logos in relation to Christ is true of the good in relation to God.

The way in which God resists equation with a general and prior norm of the good must be further clarified. A mere reference to the fact is not enough. For the extra element in God which says more than the mere norm of the good can express might be no more than a mythological margin with no significance of its own. If so, it would be desirable to set aside the margin and arrive at the norm as a purely ethical entity. For this reason we must ask what it means that the word "God" transcends the norm of the good and resists equation with this norm.

Two aspects of this question are worth noting.

(i) The good meets us in the ethical sphere only within the polarity of good and evil. To will the good, or even to think it, always means not willing the bad and thus thinking of the good as its opposite. The integration of the good into this polarity shows that we can understand ethical imperatives only as a protest. Man should not be as he is. What we ought to be involves what we ought not to be. It thus entails controversy with what we are. The negative form of the decalogue: "Thou shalt not . . . ," brings out strictly the protest character of the imperative. It has in view fallen man. It says to him: You ought not to be as you are. This negative thrust of the imperative is plain in Kant too. Man's personhood comes out in his refusal to be as he is in his conflict with the impulses, the eudaemonism, and the laissez-faire of his nature. It is the mark of his humanity that he is entangled in this conflict with himself. The more intense the conflict, the more human he is.

We cannot think of God, however, within this presupposed polarity of good and evil.

We are thus brought to the same conclusion as before. When God is fitted into an existing schema, what is outside God is the true *ens realissimum* and God is reduced to no more than a mythical term for this which sooner or later will become superfluous.

One possibility is that God will be seen as a representative of the good in this polarity. In this case evil will be an independently existing rival. God will no longer be Lord of all (cf. Marcion). He will be fitted into a polar law of being. He will be one element in the dialectic. He might be the God of Plato, who shapes pre-existent matter, but he will not be able to escape the perverse or evil element in it. He will not be God in the sense of the biblical Creator who creates out of nothing and who thus knows nothing given before or outside himself with which he must reckon and by which the law of his own action is in part controlled.

A second possibility is that God will be seen as a representative of the polarity itself, as the neutral point between the two poles. In this case he will personify the principle of teleology in the polarity. Evil will be understood as a productive transition to good (Hegel), or even as a spur to it, calling for decision and thus for the first time making good possible. Does not Goethe's Mephistopheles play this role, always willing evil but bringing about the good? Did not Schiller along these lines view the Fall as the most fortunate event in history, since it brought man out of the animal obscurity of paradise and made decision possible for him? Did not the prodigal son, according to Gide, need the far country in order to win by alienation the good of his identity?

When God, either way, is equated with a general idea, in this case the teleology of good and evil, he is put below an *ens realissimum* which is stronger than he is and which finds a place for him in the nexus of being only as a cipher for this nexus. But again we must say that the God of the Bible will not be fitted into this schematizing and will not let himself be subsumed in this way. He is not a neutral point between good and evil; his wrath rages against evil. Evil is overcome, not by being manifested in its creative finality, but in such a way that evil is pardoned instead of being explained away. Evil is overcome by love (Luke 15:20f.).

No matter whether the word "God" is equated with the good or with the polarity itself, the God of the Bible cannot be brought into congruity with either. In obvious respects he stands above both.

The God of the Bible relativizes, or, better, judges the polarity of good and evil instead of being included in it. This has the following implication.

Since God creates out of nothing, created man belongs to him totally. He must give himself back to God as he has received himself from him. If he falls into alienation and disloyalty, he cannot point in excuse to realities which are outside God's creative act and man's guilt. He cannot refer to matter and say that this drags him down and poisons his existence through no fault of his own. He cannot adduce forces of destiny which have been in the world from the outset. He is unconditionally and totally guilty before God.

Yet in seeing himself set between good and evil, he finds that the evil in him is not something that God called forth out of nothing. Mephistopheles is not his creation. God does not will the bad. Man may oppose his imperative to evil, as Kant does, but evil is in him. He is constitutionally tied to it. His acts may be one long pro- test against it, but what he protests against is part of himself. He has to say: I am the bad.

Paul can say for a moment, almost by way of experiment, that sin is a kind of mythical power which confronts him and which is not himself (Rom. 7:17, 20-23). His true self does not will sin but rejects it. If he still does it, he is mastered by a power outside himself which he does not control and for which he is not responsible. If evil is still within him, it is the supporter of another power which has penetrated the self. Yet he can say this only for a moment. At the end of the passage he says: "O wretched man that I am, who shall deliver me from the body of this death?" (7:24). Here he again says "I" to himself. He sees that the vessel which contains evil is his own body. The temporary distinction between himself and the evil seen in himself is now reversed. He has to equate himself with this evil, or, more accurately, he would have to do so if victory had not been given him through Christ, if he had not become a new creature, if he had not attained a new identity (Rom. 7:24b; 2 Cor. 5:17; Gal. 2:20).

The radicalization of the decalogue in the Sermon

on the Mount shows that I have to say Yes to the lurking
and potential evil within me. Anger means a withholding
of part of the self from God (Matt. 5:21ff.). Lust means
emancipation from the divine order even when it does not
come to physical expression (5:27ff.).

Hence I cannot say Yes merely to my ethical and
higher self, to the self which in mind and act says Yes to
the good. That against which I protest in mind and act,
even though it be below the level of control, is also part
of me (cf. Matt. 15:19; Mark 7:21; Luke 9:47; Rom.
2:15). In face of him who created the world out of nothing I can neither ascribe it to fate nor trace it back to
God as first cause. Far from being productive material
for the fulfilment of duty, potential evil is part of myself.
It does not let me belong totally to him to whom I owe
myself totally. I cannot love him with all my heart and
soul and mind (Matt. 22:27; Deut. 6:4).

A final question is thus put to the polarity of good
and evil. When the confrontation of good and evil takes
place, there can be no full orientation to God nor unequivocal being as a creature. When I see myself in God's
light I am startled by the dark possibilities within me.
For in this light I learn my true identity and this necessary self-identification is at first a crushing work of law
and judgment. I have to say "I" to that in me which God
does not will and in which I am apart from him.

If, however, the polarity of good and evil takes
God's place as the *ens realissimum*, this self-identification
ceases to be radical. For I identify myself with myself
only as a moral subject. I thus set myself apart from evil
as something that is no part of me, whether in the form
of inheritance, of environment, of destiny, or of disposi-
tions, in Kant's sense, which I need not impute to myself
and to which I need not say "I." The rule of the polarity
of good and evil means that some dimensions of the I do
not belong ethically to the person. Hence there is no radical self-identification.

We can learn from the biblical story of the Fall in

this regard. Here the serpent brings knowledge of good
and evil. When he triumphs the polarity is put in force
(Gen. 3:5). Man as created was totally oriented to God.
He lived, moved, and had his being unequivocally in him.
The hour had not yet come when autonomy awakened and
he broke free from God. He still turned to God in eternal
liturgy. Knowledge of good and evil was not yet relevant,
for evil had no actuality. Only when man ate of the tree
of knowledge of good and evil and broke God's prohibi-
tion was there knowledge of good and evil and the in-
auguration of the polarity. This knowledge comes with
the actualization of evil and man's separation from the
Creator. It is practical, not theoretical. With it man
ceases to be unequivocal and is betrayed into conflict.

In this "reverse prophecy" we have an interpretation of man's historicity. This historicity now lies within
the polarity of good and evil. But this means that man's
whole being is called in question. Even the polarity and
the fruitfulness of the conflict are marked by dark
shadows. Man is chained to the polarity. He cannot overcome himself and become another. He cannot break free
from the evil within him even in the name of a moral
imperative. The sinister mark of an alien power is always
on him. The development of a new utopian man is blocked.
An indication of this is that war can be called the father
of all things. Man can achieve his best only in frustration.
He needs contradiction. Egoism is the most powerful driv-
ing force of history and therefore of progress, although
not of progress alone.

From all this it is evident that the word "God"
denotes something more and other than the mere idea of
the good. God challenges even the good of man, for he
shows how dubious is the framework within which it appears and prevents the idealization by which the polarity
of good and evil is made into a creative impulse or a teleo-
logical principle.

Nor is it just a matter of the law by which God
calls in question the good and its whole framework. It is

also a matter of the gospel in which he brings in the new form of the good. This new form makes man unequivocal again. It is given in love as the fulfilling of the law (Rom. 13:10; cf. Matt. 19:19; 22:34-40; Mark 12:31; Gal. 5:14; James 2:8).

He who loves is wholly *in* the act of love. No dimension of the I has to be suppressed here. Hence, as Luther says, spontaneity and promptitude are proper to the act of love. If it must still be said that we have not yet attained but press on (Phil. 3:12), we still have the promise, and the history of its fulfilment has begun. I am already apprehended by Christ and hence I can apprehend him. I am loved and thus I can love in return (1 John 4:19). The fact that I am apprehended points to the basis of this possibility. Love does not have its source in an ethical act of my own. If it did, it would be located where it does not belong, namely, in the polarity of good and evil and hence in man's conflict with himself which ends when man becomes unequivocal again. In fact, however, love arises as man's response and reaction to a love which apprehends him (1 John 4:10). It is, one might say, the subjective reflection of the fact that God in Christ is a lovable object (Augsburg Confession, Apology Art. III).

Thus the word "God," transcending the good of polarity, shows us here that man is unequivocal again, that he has overcome alienation, and that he is free. For the message about God is that he discloses himself to us as love and thus makes possible my answering love. Total challenge is thus replaced by total acceptance, which we call justification. That which transcends the good in the new understanding of the word "God" points to the totality of the self which without God would slip into the necessity of conflict, a necessity which man would then idealize as a virtue and make into a substitute for the lost totality.

The word "God" transcends the good in another respect too. The love won from me, which makes me unequivocal again, leads me to my fellows. Love of God and love of neighbor are indissolubly related. Confessing Christ means recognizing him in those who need me here and now. The call of love is the claim of faith. This means that the good of turning to others can never be an act independent of faith in God, at least in the Christian sense. For as a believer I see Christ in the needy. Even though I do not like them, I see in them those whom God seeks with the same love with which he sought me, whom he forgives as he forgave me (Matt. 18:21ff.), who are bought with a price as I am (Rom. 14:15; 1 Cor. 8:11).

My fellows are thus transformed for me. They have an alien dignity which comes from God. They can no longer be merely used (even ethically), whether in the sense of being there for him that he might be there for me (Matt. 5:46f.), or in the sense of serving my self-fulfilment (cf. Wilhelm von Humboldt).

God as Lord of neighborly love transcends the ethical motif and its good in this area too. He does so because with his initiative of love he gives my fellows meaning as neighbors, qualifies afresh my natural love, and makes it impossible for me to leave him out at any later stage in life. Faith in God cannot be just an introduction to this form of humanity which can later be replaced by atheistic humanism, by the humanism of a general proclamation of human dignity. Dogmatics and ethics are also indissolubly related. Faith cannot be lost in fellow-humanity, for the meaning of the fellow-man is grounded in this faith and the word "God" always defines the word "man" in this sense.

This is the factor in the word "God" which transcends every good, including our turning to our fellows.

(ii) The transcendent factor in the word "God" in relation to the good may be seen not only in God's distinction from the polarity of ethical good and evil but also in the fact that I can never reach God by seeking him in the name of the good. To understand this we must turn again to the story of the rich young ruler.

We have seen already that the ruler is asking after God when he asks about eternal life, that is, life in fellowship with God. And he thinks he will find an answer if he can learn what the good is which by doing he will secure union with God (Matt. 19:16ff.). It is worth noting how Jesus makes it plain that the question, as thus posed, bypasses God, or, better, how God is above this type of inquiry.

To be sure, Jesus seems at first to accept the question as the young man puts it. For he answers by referring to the commandments: "If you would enter life, keep the commandments" (v. 17). The ruler's reply that he has done this, so what more is needed (v. 20), shows that he has taken the ethical path in vain. Jesus was clearly aiming in Socratic fashion at this response. His method makes recognition of the futility of the ethical path particularly acute.

Why is this way futile? Why does it bypass God?

The answer emerges from Jesus' demand: "If you would be perfect, go, sell what you possess and give to the poor, and you will have treasure in heaven; and come, follow me" (v. 21). But the young man "went away sorrowful; for he had great possessions" (v. 22).

With his demand that the young man sell all his goods, Jesus closes, again Socratically, the way of the commandments or the ethical way. He forces on the ruler an experiment of thought. This young man must ask how unconditional is his concern for eternal life and God. Is his interest a philosophical one that does not have to be satisfied? Does he want to fill an urgent but not intolerable gap in life? Or in the search for God is he raising the supreme question of life and destiny? Is this a venture by whose success or failure he will stand or fall? Only if his question has this radical quality is he really asking after God. If he is, he sees that the gaining of eternal life is the one thing necessary (Luke 10:42), and that to miss it is no less than total disaster. If not, then God is simply one among many questions, like an eleventh commandment. He has an additional commandment of this kind in view when he asks about new forms of the good which go beyond his existing list of duties.

The ruler's decision how he wants God, as a radical or an incidental matter, necessarily has to be taken and declared once Jesus tells him to sell all that he has. The experiment of thought which is forced on him takes the following form.

He has to say which is more important, his property, social prestige, culture, and life-style, or the question of eternal life and God. If property, or self, is more important, then he has not really put the question of God at all, and he can obviously find no answer to a question which has not been put. He has not really had in view the good about which he seemed to be asking. He was thinking only of an ethical quantity which he had to augment by increased effort. He did not have the authentic good in mind as it is defined by God himself, namely, as self-giving, an unconditional and unreserved being there for others.

The rich young ruler is not ready for the challenge and hence he goes away sadly, for he has many possessions. He tries to ask about the good and God without being prepared for self-sacrifice. Hence he never really asks at all. He is confounded not merely by the denial of an answer but by his own question.

I can ask about God, and about the meaning of the word "God," only on two conditions. First, I must not think in terms of my own idea of the good, that is, ethical achievement, but in terms of what the good is that is in and by God: One alone is good. Secondly, I can ask radically about the good, this good and therefore God, only if I ask not in uncommitted if serious curiosity, but in the unconditional readiness and commitment which understands God as the one and all: "When you seek me with all your heart, I will be found by you" (Jer. 29:13f.; cf. Deut. 4:29). If God is love, he can be asked after only in the same situation of love and self-giving. This is not possible if the heart is divided and the will torn: I cannot love God and mammon (Luke 16:13); I cannot love God and self. This is why the Gentiles in Romans 1:18ff. miss the question of God. They do not lack speculative drive. They have their own ethos. But they are fixed on themselves and therefore they do not honor God or give him thanks. Theology, which has to do with the Theos, can be pursued only in a specific orientation of existence. Only he who is of the truth, who wills God unequivocally, hears his voice.

## 3. Results and Evaluation

(1) The question of God ends in the void if it starts with the assumption that God is identical with my idea of the good or is just a cipher for it.

(2) On the other hand the true good which is God himself and which transcends my idea of it is not under my control. If God himself is the good, I can know it only when he discloses himself to me. This self-disclosure, however, cannot mean that I am given a doctrine about God's being and nature. It means that my existence is brought into the truth and is changed into one of self-giving and openness to God. This miracle of change is called in the Bible the work of the Holy Spirit. For the Spirit reveals what flesh and blood can never tell themselves (Matt. 16:17). He also gives the mind which opens us to what is disclosed. He accomplishes the miracle of the new birth (John 3:3, 5). He brings into being the new creature (2 Cor. 5:17). He sets us in new life (Rom. 7:8). He changes life both noetically and ontically (cf. his lifegiving role as the *ruach* or breath of God (Gen. 2:7; Ps. 104:29f.; 146:5; Eccl. 12:7). This new existence, which I cannot give myself, is marked by the fact that my concern is with God alone, that I want him unconditionally, and that I can reach him with my question, whereas otherwise I miss him and understand him merely

as the cipher of a norm, a value, or a telos of my old existence.

(3) The fact that the new disposition is not under our control shows that the question of eternal life and of God is not a question of the natural man or an expression of his religious interest. The conclusion of the story of the rich young ruler makes this point. He asked after God in a frame of mind which prevented him from really having God in view. Hence he missed God. He could not help this, for the natural constitution of our existence does not permit us to move out of the circle of the self and self-love. Hence we can ask only after a God who is compatible with our self-love, who does not challenge it, who does not call us out of the conditions of our previous existence. Hence we have here something that is "impossible with men" (Matt. 19:26). God himself is the only possibility of breaking through this closed circle. By nature, man sets up a false God by deifying the creature. This God, being only a cipher, fits in smoothly, exerts no pressure, and offers no radical challenge. For a reality which is identical with itself—in this case the reality of the creaturely—cannot call itself in question (cf. Luther's Larger Catechism, First Commandment).

(4) But is it not pointless to demonstrate the meaning of the word "God" in a general way? Does not the meaning emerge only when the disposition that is not under our control becomes an event?

This is a good question to the extent that God cannot be demonstrated apart from the disposition that becomes an event. The failure of the proofs of God shows this. This failure is not just epistemological (in the Kantian sense). It is connected with the fact that when existence emancipates itself from God it is no longer apt for the reality of God and is robbed of the truth of its being. Hence the question behind the proofs misses God. Anselm saw this very well in his misnamed proof of God.

To explain the word "God" generally can only bring to light the difference between God and all other concepts (including that of meaning or of the good). This does not have to mean that in this area we can speak of God only negatively, simply saying what he is not. We have also to consider what it implies that there is this difference. We have done this in relation to meaning and the good, trying to show how far meaning and the good do not answer man's quest for the transcendent but rivet him to himself.

The difference of God from these values and norms reflects another difference, namely, the difference between man's knowledge that he is a being that reaches beyond itself, that cannot accept itself as given, that has to see and develop itself in relation to something, and his knowledge (suppressed, according to Rom. 1:18) that the goals which he selects do not in fact transcend him. For these goals are taken from his given reality. They are idols which simply play the role of deified creation and a religious superstructure.

This difference can be the theme of general discussion. Its implications can be considered. Hence reflections on the meaning of the word "God" are legitimate. They are one of the many forms in which the believer bears witness to the logos of his hope and develops it as logos (1 Pet. 3:15f.), showing to everybody (not just to Christians and fellow-believers) that what he says about God is responsible talk, that he means something by the word "God," and that this is not just a traditional and thoughtless cliche.

This is, of course, all that general reflection on the word "God" can achieve. It does not amount to a proof of God. Even when the logos is penetrating, it is simply a Christian idea of God and no more than a shadow of the reality. Whether reality attaches to it or not remains an open question. Whether we are dealing with Immanuel, with the God for me whom I can trust with all my heart, cannot be known. Decisive access to God takes place when we have to do with more and other than mere insight into the meaningful nature of the concept, when we have the disposition of existence which is the work of the Spirit.

Nevertheless, it is a constant and significant task, in the vestibule of faith, to clarify what is meant by the word "God." For only in so doing can he who proclaims and confesses God make it clear that he is not claiming special revelation or engaging only in traditional patter —both of which would be obstacles to his hearers—but is speaking in solidarity with the world of reason in thus giving an account of the logos of what he says.

(5) The fact that God differs from and transcends all the norms and values implicit in our questions is shown in most of the dialogues of Jesus. When Jesus is asked about eternal life, or who is the greatest (Mark 9:33ff.; Matt. 18:1f.), or whether taxes should be paid to Caesar (Matt. 22:15ff.), or who is my neighbor (Luke 10:29, 36), or how often one should forgive others (Matt. 18:21ff.), he never gives a direct answer. For if a direct answer were given it would be under the control of the question. The question, however, comes from the old existence. In this dimension the answer could not bear appropriate witness to God. Hence a counterquestion follows instead of an answer, as in the story of the rich young ruler. This counterquestion, which does not have to be put in question form, but may be Socratically indirect, has a revelatory function. It shows how inadequate is the disposition from which the question derives. The question as put has to be corrected. Man has to see that he himself is questioned by God. The original question: "Where is God?" has to be replaced by the reverse and prior question: "Adam, where art thou?" (Gen. 3:9).

(6) If in view of his distinction from all norms and values God is the ground of all things, no ground can be found for him. Here reason is brought to silence, since its function is to find grounds. Yet this situation is not irrational, since we can see that no ground can be found for what is the ground of all else. We are indeed summoned to think of this ground of all things when what we try to grasp by way of immanent grounds does not do

justice to man as a being that transcends itself, but makes him a mere function of these grounds and thus robs him of his unconditionality.

All this may be merely the obscure sign of a remote power, but a sign is still set up. When we come to God's revelation or self-disclosure, the obscure sign is replaced by the "I am" and the questionable good is replaced by him who is good. This is why the final basis of the commandments lies in the recurrent liturgical statement: "I am the Lord your God" (Num. 19:2, 4, 10, 18, etc.). The author of the law does not legitimate himself by the meaningful character of his laws. His laws are legitimated and grounded by the author for whom no ground may be sought or found.

This is where the leap is made over the barrier between the norms, values, and false gods of religious man and the self-disclosing "I am" of God. Reflection on the meaning of the word "God" can only survey this barrier and that which it both separates and connects.

The most important result of our discussion is this. Although God relates to all dimensions of human life, although we learn something of the meaning of being and history from him, although he may be known in his connection with the good, although he has to do with our love and freedom, he is not identical with any of these things but stands in infinitely qualitative distinction from them.

Christian theology has always been brought up against this distinction by the fact that the terms it uses to describe God, and especially the Trinity, are inadequate for the task. Hence the terms logos, nature, person, substance, and so forth, have to undergo a shift in meaning. Their content has to be filled out by what they are supposed to express. This means that the doctrine of God cannot be worked out deductively. We cannot move on from the meaning of *persona* to the personality of God or from that of substance to the monotheistic structure of Christian faith in God. The normal use can only lead to the God of the philosophers and drop the elements which are beyond a mere extension of our experience of life and the world. The terms we use have to play a servant role. Their use has to be instrumental. As in the case of logos in John's Gospel, a new content has to replace the old one—a content which the original meaning could not foresee.

Yet the new definition within the sphere of the word "God" does not mean that every connection with the original meaning is broken. The Stoic sense of Logos is caught up in the new definition in John. If this were not possible, if the terms bore no relation to what they mean theologically and christologically, they could be arbitrarily changed. Indeed, articulate concepts would no longer exist. We should be reduced to glossolalia. As one might say, the vocabulary of faith adopts the language prepared in the theater (cf. *persona*), philosophy, and common usage. But the terms have to be baptized or converted before they can render their appointed service. No term can fully express God. This is one reason why the Bible always speaks of the name of God rather than the concept of God. For the personal name expresses uniqueness. He who bears a name cannot be subsumed under a species. He is unchangeably and inexchangeably himself, as we shall see later.

The mere concept "God" means nothing by itself. It is theologically empty. It can be used only to denote an exalted and numinous creaturely reality. As a mere word, "God" cannot denote what we have described as God's distinction from all creaturely reality. It may express an unconditional relation to God or it may be taken mechanically from religious tradition. In this sense Tillich is right when he says that it can be atheism to affirm God's existence as well as to deny it.

In modern theological discussion this is the point of the interest in the relevance of God. The social and broader ethical relations of the word "God" are sought. Out of concern lest the word be a mere cliche or shibboleth, God is not accepted as one who stands over against us personally, for example, as the one to whom prayer is addressed. He is sought immanently, for instance, in our fellow-men. An attempt is made to make him intelligible to modern man, who supposedly will accept only what is immanent. The distinction is erased in the interests of mission.

But this is done at an irresponsibly high cost, namely, the whole point of the word "God" in the Christian sense. We thus have a relapse into paganism. Creaturely relations are deified. The way is thus prepared for thoroughgoing secularism. When reason reads the open text, it can dispense with God as a cipher of fellow-humanity. If theology simply says what the world can say to itself, it says nothing. The feet of those who will remove it are at the door. The attractive packaging of the word "God" to promote a boom in sales is simply a selling out at reduced prices.

The word "God" does not derive its vitality from its affinity to creaturely dimensions but from its distinction from them. To overlook the affinity is to relapse into a docetic theism or outworn traditionalism. To overlook the distinction is to lead through a transitional phase, when journalists and intellectuals admire the courage of these pioneers, to the complete autarchy of self-enclosed, and in reality atheistic, secularism. The alarm caused when a secular God is first proclaimed, and catches brief attention, passes quickly. The stillness of a world which can understand itself without this God closes over him. What is self-evident quickly spends itself.

Röhricht in his *Leben angesichts des Todes* (1968, pp. 175ff.) rightly takes issue with Bonhoeffer's thesis that God is not to be sought in the gaps but in the center of life. Man lives in time, guilt, finitude, and the certainty of death (p. 175). Hence his reality is in question. How can he hear the Word of God in it? Does not his experience of God correspond to his experience of the deficiencies in life? Is not the affinity to God obvious here

(p. 177)? One can accept this so long as one adds that the experience of deficiencies does not lead necessarily to God. It may lead to the experience of absurdity, as in Camus, or to declaration of the principle of hope, as in Bloch, for whom the *ens realissimum* takes the temporal form of a utopian end.

Thus the experience of want is ambivalent. It may be either open or closed to God. It can even be open to God in deceptive fashion. This is what Bonhoeffer seems to have had in view. We can paint this world in darker colors in order to heighten the radiance of the heavenly Jerusalem. We can sing of this world as a vale of woe in order to make heaven the more desirable. The deception here is that God becomes no more than the expression of our wishful thinking and can thus be interpreted as an illusion along the lines of Feuerbach.

A reversal is thus demanded. Experience of God must come first to show us what is really missing in human existence. I learn the fulness of love, and the lovelessness and selfishness of human life, only from the God who is present in Christ. It is he who shows me the unity of power and love and therewith their separation in human history.

When what I experience of the deficiencies in human life is related to God, it is altered not by correction but by the fact that man is transformed into a new creature. Supplementing and correcting is my own work. Transforming, however, has to be done *on* me.

## 4. The Personality of God and the Problem of the Word "Person" as a Theological Category

The word "person" is our best defense against the ideas and postulates which have led to the God of the philosophers. For it denotes an individuality that cannot be subsumed. It still poses a problem, of course, in other respects. For does not individuality mean limitation? Is it not a threat, then, to the deity of God?

Again, the description of God as personal is suggested by the fact that God is not just an answer to human questions. In his self-revelation he gives the disposition for asking after him. He brings us into the truth. With the new creature he introduces new questions. Hence the who or what of God can hardly be expressed except by the word person. For as person he is never an object, for example, the object of our questions, hopes, and so on. He is always self-disclosing and acting subject. This concept is needed to express the fact that God is understanding, freedom, and love. He is not just a first cause. He is the Creator who gives man his own being with the power to decide whether or not to take up his destiny as God's partner.

The concept of person raises problems, so that Tillich thinks it better not to speak of the personal God but to refer instead to the ground of being. In view of what has been said, it must be admitted that the application of personal terms to God has its doubtful side. As we have shown, the word "God" can never be a synonym for other words such as norm, value, and so on, but always transcends them. The same is true of person. Equating God and person, or even trying to use the human person as a model for the idea of God, is ruled out from the very first. For this would be to make God in the image of the creature as in human religion and idolatry. God as an old gentleman with a long beard is an extreme instance of this. When the personal character of God is controlled by the picture of man there can be no evading the verdict of anthropomorphism.

We may thus say that as Christ is not to be defined by the Logos concept, but himself defines the content of this, so God is not to be defined by a prior concept of person, but must give this a new content when it is pressed into service to describe his nature.

Hence two steps must be taken. We must show positively how the concept is suitable when we are speaking about God. We must then show negatively how it is unsuitable.

### (1) *The Suitability of the Concept*

The suitability of the concept may be seen first from theologies which emphatically reject it. A. E. Biedermann in right-wing Hegelianism and D. F. Strauss in left-wing Hegelianism are examples. For them God is the absolute Spirit and the finite spirit is simply a transition in the process of self-knowledge. Hence person and personality simply express an inferior and inadequate religious notion. Since Hegel in some sense sets the absolute and finite Spirit on the same plane, that is, that of self-development, he works out the classical schema of thought within which God is integrated into the human concept and thus ceases to transcend it. Rejection of the idea of person along such lines might well serve to commend it.

In fact, the transcendent element in God which is above all concepts is well expressed whenever God is spoken of as person.

(i) To say that God is person means that he cannot be an object of our thought—natural theology leads only to religious man—nor an object of our ethical striving—this leads only to a righteousness of works. Instead, God is a free subject working on and in us and leading us into the truth in which we can hear his voice and orient our willing and doing to him (Phil. 2:13).

This means, of course, that only a specific aspect of the concept of person can be used to express the nature of God. It cannot in its whole range be congruent with, or normative for, that which is denoted by the word "God." Barth rightly contends for this limited use of the word "person" when he says that the real issue is not that God has personality but that he is the one who loves. What counts is not that he is person but what kind of person he is. Here is the essential point whether or not the terms personality or person are used. Again, personal attributes may be freely used even though one is aware that to talk this way, as always in theology, is simply to use the terms available without allowing them to become dominant or normative. Along these lines the word "person" serves to show that God is free subject in a free address of love.

(ii) The word "person" can also be of service from another angle. By nature the person is always in relation to a Thou, to another person. In this regard the concept of person corrects the concept of substance and the substantial unity of God in older trinitarian ontology. Genesis 1:26 suggests the relational character of the word "person" when it has God say: "Let us make man . . ." This "we" forms the framework of Johannine christology.

Thus when Jesus says that the Son can do nothing of himself (John 5:19, 20), he is describing his person as one of relation to the Father. Indeed, the very terms "Father" and "Son" imply this relation. The Father is Father only in relation to the Son and *vice versa*. Neither is a self-centered entelechy. Each is there for and to the other. The monadic concept of substance is inadequate, therefore, to describe the relation of God and Christ as the unity of the divine essence. Their oneness is misunderstood if it is seen as a static unity, which is all that the concept of substance can suggest.

Here the concept of person comes in as a corrective. The Son relates to the Father. He is not self-centered. He constantly gives himself. He is one with the Father and lives a dialogical, not a monological, existence.

The concept of person also has a part to play with reference to man. As he is one with the Father, so Christ in his high-priestly prayer asks that his own may be one in him (John 17:11, 21f.). As he can do nothing without the Father, so his own can do nothing without him (John 15:5). They, too, are not alone; they are to him and from him. To the extent that person means being in relation to the Thou, the personal category can best express this.

Even when the word is applied to God himself, this relational element is claimed. God determines himself as Immanuel, as God for man, for his people, for the world (cf. John 3:16f.; 12:47; 8:12; 9:5; 2 Cor. 5:19; 1 Tim. 1:15; 1 John 4:14). In the first commandment he gives himself to be known as "my" Lord and God. He is the Lord of the covenant. He establishes it freely as a covenant (*diatheke*). He is not just the partner in a contract (*syntheke*) which exists apart from him.

That God freely binds himself to man as Immanuel, holding nothing back (Luther), may be seen in the fact that he speaks, that he utters his Word, and that he does this in free sovereignty. "He is the Lord of the verbal character of His Word" (Barth, CD, I, 1, p. 157). When the Word is made flesh, his condescension, his dialogical solidarity with man, reaches its peak. Encountering us in his Word, entering into it although not being enclosed by it (cf. Deut. 31:18; Job 13:24; Prov. 1:28; Jer. 14:8f.; 15:18; 23:23; and Calvin's doctrine of the Word as always outside as well as in the flesh), he also makes those whom he addresses capable of word. He gives them answerable or responsible existence. He commands response in the form of trust and obedience and prayer: "Seek ye my face" (Ps. 27:8).

The fact that man achieves dialogical existence through the Word of God (M. Buber) points again to the personal factor which we have in view here.

In the medium of the Word, God and man are related as I and Thou, as persons. Human personality has its basis here. What other basis can there be for it than that it is referred to God's inviolable majesty by whose Word it, too, is made capable of word? If we now mean by personality the unconditionality of man which separates him from things and animals, which makes him inviolable and protects him against becoming a mere means to an end, the rank of the human proclaimed herein is grounded in what the Old Testament sayings about the image of God tell us about man's participation in the majesty of God. When this alien dignity, this existence in relation to God, is forgotten, the infinite worth implied in the concept of person is replaced by self-alienation in the sense of a purely instrumental rank.

Even when the modern understanding of the person goes back to Greek antiquity rather than the Bible, man is still related to the gods and is not an autonomous entelechy. In Greek antiquity, too, man is theonomous. In Homer man is mortal in distinction from the immortal gods. Pindar warns against trying to be as Zeus. Odysseus in Sophocles' *Ajax* recognizes that all who live are but empty shadows. Vergil's Aeneas is the pious hero. Horace says that we reign because we bow to the gods. Plato argues that God, not man, is the measure of all things. Modern humanism cannot be understood apart from this origin and background.

(iii) A further element in the concept of person is that the person can never be reduced to a concept but always resists such reduction. This finds ample illustration in the human sphere.

Personal identity is obscured when people are referred to in numbers or material terms. To reduce them to a concept or type is to rob them of their true being, as Max Frisch constantly insists.

H. Braun thinks that the concept of person is a modern and not a biblical construct and that it is thus inadequate to indicate God. But when in a television discussion he once tried to embarrass Goppelt by asking him to translate the word "person" into Hebrew, Goppelt unhesitatingly offered *shem*, the Hebrew word for name.

It is in fact a remarkable point that persons have names to express their non-interchangeable identity. The identity denoted by names refuses to accept any other definition. Great difficulty is caused when people have to be identified by purely external characteristics or subjective impressions as at an interview. Might not the person be very different at another time or to other people, for example, relatives, colleagues, or rivals? Any attempt to equate someone with a role or to subsume someone under a concept leads to distortion of his or her uniqueness. This uniqueness is a transcendent factor, a free possibility which cannot be pinned down.

It is expressed by the name. The name evades the concept. A concept is a fixed designation. It takes up a thing, process, idea, or norm into the meaning which it denotes and grasps it. But the name is not a designation of this kind. In itself it says nothing. When I do not know someone, or know someone only by accounts of him, his name gives me no idea of him. Conversations about whom people have married and what has become of them are boring if these people are only names to us. Even when the names are expanded to denote certain features, for example, Charles the Great, the additions are still separate from the name itself, except in the Bible when names themselves are originally given to denote the person (cf. Matt. 1:21; 16:18; Mark 3:16; Luke 9:54f.; Acts 4:36; 13:8; Phil. 2:9; also Gen. 17:5, 15, and Ruth 1:20). The name can normally be filled out and interpreted only by the one who bears it.

Now as I encounter people I constantly find myself relating names to concepts. This person is a typical manager or is typically ambitious or phlegmatic. This is to subsume people under concepts which do not do justice to them. In doing this I rob them of the possibility of being themselves and of representing the extra element which is in open development.

For this reason, only the name can do justice to selfhood in its non-interchangeability. The one who bears a name is not defined but presented. He presents himself. That is, he opens a history with himself in which he discloses or hides his true self but in which this true self is always relevant. In contrast, mere mention of his name, as in a telephone directory, tells us nothing about him.

The name in its uniqueness, a uniqueness which is still valid even when the name is a common one, is thus the privilege of the person. It opposes subsumption under a universal. It expresses non-identity with anyone else.

In personal dealings the name also serves to

identify others. This does not mean that the name as such opens up the secret of others. It simply tells us who is under discussion. Only by self-declaration can this person show us in part who he or she really is.

This role of the name in personal dealings is brought out by the fact that names are mostly given by others. When someone chooses his own name, it is still for the sake of others, not for his own sake. This function of the name corresponds to the nature of the person, which exists in being for the Thou, in communication, not solipsistically for the self.

These characteristics of the name make it clear for the first time why the name of God represents his personhood, that is, why the word "person" can in some dimensions of its meaning be used to describe God. When God declares his name, he shows that he cannot be located in the nexus of being. He is not part of something all-embracing. He cannot be subsumed under something higher or other. He is unique. Beside him there are no gods (Exod. 15:11; 23:13; Ps. 86:8; 96:4, etc.). He also shows himself as the one who wills to be Immanuel, who demands obedience, who wants to be invoked. In short, he binds himself to man in speech and answer, in personal dialogue.

This is what is meant by God's manifesting himself as Yahweh at the burning bush in Exodus 3:14: "I will be who I will be." This cannot be meant as a self-definition. It cannot be an antipersonal act. For God does not lay down his nature and conduct in this name. He leaves everything open. He himself will in the future reveal who he is and will be. There is thus declared the freedom of the self-manifesting God for future self-manifestation and self-impartation in history. The name does not give full information about the nature. It simply shows who is under discussion, leaving it to God himself to reveal himself, to interpret his name by what he says and does in self-manifestation. The only thing laid down by the name Yahweh is that the self-revelation and self-impartation will follow and that an infinite number of possible modes of speech and action are at God's disposal. Along these lines the "I am" and "I will be" mean "I am there for you." The "being" in the name of Yahweh is not to be construed as "self-being" but as "being for."

From two further angles we may see how little Yahweh has here the function of pinning down God conceptually.

First, the self-naming "I will be who I will be" is not a namegiving in the sense that it can be grasped in the form of a picture, likeness, or concept. From that standpoint it is more a veiling or the refusal of a name. Moses is asking what he shall say when he tells the children of Israel that the God of their fathers has sent him and they ask: "What is his name?" But he receives no true answer to this question, at least not the kind of answer which the question as to the name implies. For did they not want to know the name of God in order to take possession of it? In opposition to this the name of Yahweh has an ironical twist: "I am who I am—ready," or, to put it in the future which Hebrew scholars prefer: "You will soon see from the history begun by me who I am and as whom I will make myself known."

Is Yahweh an answer to the question of God's name? Is the answer "I will be who I will be" a name which is analogous to other divine names and which might be put on a list of the gods? Is it not a retreat from apprehension by name? Is it not in the true sense a promise? A promise which leaves everything open and out of which a mosaic of the picture of God can be formed? Are we not referred to future possibilities of God which he reserves for himself, so that he alone knows himself and will reveal this knowledge only by his acts?

Not just the concept of person, but the name especially designed for God is not, then, a simple synonym which exhausts God. Even the name has a final incommensurability which means that God escapes and transcends it. Although different, the name still shares the ambivalence of all concepts which try to grasp God's nature and forcefully to subsume it under something superior. The fact that the name can be used to gain power over God is expressed precisely in the refusal of a name. The author is obviously aware of magical misuse bound up with names, that is, the acquiring of power and the employment in spells and incantations. Hence the transcendence of Yahweh evades even the name.

This may be seen again when Jacob wrestles with God at Jabbok. He asks God for his name but the only answer is: "Why is it that you ask my name? And he blessed him there" (Gen. 32:29). Yahweh makes himself known through blessing, not through his name. Similarly Manoah is told in Judges 13:18: "Why do you ask my name, seeing it is wonderful?"

Secondly, the refusal of God to let the name Yahweh be a means of grasping him conceptually may be seen in the mutation which this name undergoes in the Septuagint. For here the name becomes an ontological concept of being. "I will be who I will be" becomes "I am he who truly is." Thus the refusal of a name which projected God's mystery and pointed to future disclosures yields to a conceptual definition. This definition fits God's nature into a non-historical ontological concept and thus subsumes it. If even the name, which has some suitability in distinction from the concept, can still undergo alienation in this way, the alienation becomes total confusion once the name is again allotted conceptual functions.

### (2) *The Unsuitability of the Concept*

Our attempt to clarify the meaning of the word "person" as a term for God has constantly brought us up against the limit set for the possibilities of this term. As has been seen, it can take on the function of a concept and thus become incapable of expressing what we mean by the personal God. For when we say this, we have in mind the God who discloses himself to us in free address by his Word, who thus makes us capable of word and to that extent answerable, and who thus lets us have a share in the dignity of personhood as an I, over against the divine Thou. If this and this alone is what is meant when we use the word "person" for God, only some parts of its signification are applicable to God. The word "person" is not a comprehensive one into which God can be fitted. It is, in some of its senses, a servant concept.

When we ask in what respects "person" is an inadequate term for God we note, with no surprise, that it is deficient when instead of being defined by God it is supposed to define God and therefore to be illegitimately normative. In modern philosophy, M. Scheler offers a classical example of this. He contends for a personal God, but at the cost of making an ontological concept of person the normative model for his philosophical view of God.

If we start with a prior concept of person and make it a norm, we miss the personal God of the Bible. We do so—and Fichte is right here—because we cannot think of personality and consciousness apart from limitation and finitude. An infinite person is a contradiction in terms. Communication between I and Thou is possible only because we are limited. We talk because we do not know what the other will say. We work together because there are limits to our activities and powers. We inquire because our knowledge is partial. We are always striving because we never have the whole. We feel the ethical imperative because we are never congruent with what we should be. Human personal life is possible only because of the limits and barriers between I and Thou and I and the world.

This is why Tillich cannot accept a personal God and calls the idea misleading. God cannot be *a* person. The personal element in him is that he is the ground of personhood, the bearer of its ontological power. We must not make him an individual being when he is being itself. But what remains when he is only being and not the personal other he determines to be? Can "heart" be ascribed to being? Can the basis of the world have love and understanding? Does the depth of being speak? Tillich rules out "person" as a term for God because he wishes on the basis of his view of being to set up an ontological system in which person and God represent different references of being in fixed relation to, and distance from, each other. The system makes it impossible for him to define person by God and to put it into service as thus defined.

In terms of the servant function of the word "person" it is biblically possible to claim certain elements in it. Thus God does not just call himself the ground of being from whom all the powers derive and who embraces them all. He does this (cf. Col. 1:16), but he also delimits himself from the powers as though he had limits (cf. Exod. 15:11; Deut. 32:39; 1 Kings 18:21-40; 1 Chron. 16:25; Ps. 18:11; 72:18f.; 82:1; 86:8; 96:4; 1 Cor. 12:16). As God he sets himself in comparison and accepts a point of comparison between himself and the gods. Naturally, there is some irony here. For it is only in virtue of all too human ideas that a common level is found. From God's standpoint the gods are nothing (Jer. 10:8; 16:19; Isa. 41:29). Hence it makes no sense to declare God's superiority over them or even to say that to him alone does the title God properly apply.

This simply confirms the fact that the word "person" too relates to our ideas and that only some aspects of it can be used. Even that is possible only when the aim of this use is kept in view and we avert any revolt of the conceptual means, that is, when the concept is not accorded normative rank.

In conclusion we may formulate as follows the principles for a proper theological use of the word "person."

Calling God a person does not mean transferring to God an ontological concept of person derived from man. The self-disclosing divine I makes the human Thou its personal counterpart. As only some elements in the idea of person can be used to describe God, the reverse is true. The way in which we describe God as personal or as the personal God can be applied only partially to the way in which we speak of man as a person. In this regard

God's personhood has ontic primacy over man's. When we speak of God as a person we do not mean this anthropomorphically, but when we call man a person we do mean it theomorphically.

This brings us to a final point. If the word "God" will not be subsumed under any other, if it transcends all concepts and names, even those specifically related to it, if it refuses to be a cipher for anything else, we can understand the dominant biblical statements about God, namely, that he is proclaimed in the record of history, in the account of salvation occurrence, even in stories. The unlimited character of the divine name is manifested in the flow of history which leads always to a new future. Here is the time and place of possibility in which this name constantly opens itself and keeps itself open. Here it steps forth and reveals itself and here also it retreats and keeps its mystery. Here God is both revealed and hidden (cf. Ps. 77:19; Exod. 33:23).

This unrestricted character, this reversing of possibility, is the sign of his revelation. It corresponds exactly to the name Yahweh: "I will be who I will be." God is to be found in the acts which he keeps for his freedom, which are his possibility alone, and which can never be forced into the necessity of a concept or a view of the course of history.

For this reason all that happens in the Bible is also prophecy. It refers to God's future possibilities and to the unlimited and inconceivable nature of the now. This is why we cannot have God as an idea but can only hear of him and receive him in the form of stories. We do this in recollection, re-presenting the past (Exod. 12:26; 13:14; Deut. 6:20) and remembering his mighty acts (Acts 2:11). We also do it in expectation, trusting his promise and looking toward his open possibilities. Nor are these possibilities leaps into the unknown. For he will be the same forever (Heb. 13:8; 1 Pet. 1:25; 2 John 2). With every new step he is still the God who manifested himself at the burning bush.